Praise for *The Empow*

"This book is a treasure trove of practical information addressing virtually every issue that comes up with aging parents. Linda Fodrini-Johnson is among the eldercare professionals whose advice and insights I trust the most."

—**Leslie Kernisan,** MD MPH, Founder of Better Health While Aging and author of *When Your Aging Parent Needs Help: A Geriatrician's Step-by-Step Guide to Memory Loss, Resistance, Safety Worries, & More*

"This is an incredible book written by the foremost national expert in geriatric care management. The tangible examples empower tackling some of the biggest challenges in caring for our aging loved ones. This is a must-read."

—**Matt Neal,** MBA, Chief Development Officer, Home Care Assistance

"*The Empowered Caregiver* is an excellent resource—thoughtfully organized to answer the real questions adult children of aging parents have. It gets right to the meat of the problems with kindness and compassion. Chock full of tips, checklists, and resources, Fodrini-Johnson's book expertly guides people through the many emotionally complex issues caregivers face. I plan on using this book as a resource for my clients and in my own relationship with my parents."

—**Kathryn Schofield,** elder law attorney

"Linda Fodrini-Johnson has taken her decades of experience in counseling and working with individuals and families who needed care and identified sound, useful, and important advice and actions for children of aging/ill parents. You will be empowered by her insights about difficult conversations; hospitalization preparation and discharge; safety; family-member relationships; caregiver stress, anger, and guilt; end-of-life palliative-and-hospice-care decisions; and many more challenges. This book is equally useful for caregivers of aging/ill loved ones who may not be one's parents. Each chapter has practical advice, suggested questions, and even scripts, and ends with a beautiful affirmation that is an essential self-care tool. Thank you, Linda, for organizing your experience, knowledge, and wisdom, and sharing it with those of us coping with aging loved ones."

—**Catherine Dodd**, PhD, RN, board member of the National Committee to Preserve Social Security and Medicare; member of the Expert Panel on Aging of the American Academy of Nursing; President Clinton Appointee; former board member of the Zen Hospice Project; former member of the Bay Area Task Force on Palliative Care and End of Life; Vice-Chair Commonweal Board of Directors, Policy Advisor for CA-Alliance of Nurses for Healthy Environments

"I highly recommend *The Empowered Caregiver* to anyone struggling to navigate the difficult journey of caring for an aging parent. This book offers compassionate strategies and emotional support to the caregiver, as well as provides guidance to preserve a loved one's dignity."

—**Linda Randall**, Family Caregiver

"*The Empowered Caregiver* is a must-read for any person caring for a disabled or older adult. The book has great to-do lists, sample scripts on how to start conversations, and wonderful affirmations at the end of each chapter. The author uses practical and effective tips for all types of situations. With or without any knowledge of caring for older adults, one will surely use this guide over and over again."

—**Mary Lynn Pannen,** RN, CCMC, Past President of Aging Life Care Association and Founder of Sound Options, a care management and home care firm

"This book is a must-read for anyone navigating the care of an aging family member and all of the emotions that come with it—worry, confusion, overwhelm, frustration, and guilt. Linda provides practical tips, sample scripts, and useful checklists that you can incorporate along the way. She will support you in setting limits and finding ways to accept help. With Linda, you are not alone!"

—**Lisa Mayfield,** Principal with Aging Wisdom and Past President of the Aging Life Care Association

"The Empowered Caregiver is a timely and practical guide. Linda provides bite-sized, simple advice for caregivers that makes the often-complex, daunting task of caregiving less overwhelming and manageable."

—**Grace Liu,** LCSW, Age Well Counseling

The Empowered Caregiver

Practical Advice *and* Emotional Support *for* Adult Children *of* Aging Parents

LINDA FODRINI-JOHNSON

RIVER GROVE
BOOKS

Published by River Grove Books
Austin, TX
www.rivergrovebooks.com

Distributed by River Grove Books

Design and composition by Greenleaf Book Group
Cover design by Greenleaf Book Group and Mimi Bark
Cover images used under license from ©Shutterstock.com/BK666; ©Shutterstock.com/yvonnestewarthenderson; ©Shutterstock.com/Wei xiao

Publisher's Cataloging-in-Publication data is available.

Print ISBN: 978-1-63299-425-7

eBook ISBN: 978-1-63299-426-4

First Edition

I dedicate this to my entire family, especially my mother Bernice Bidwell, who modeled care to others with an open and accepting heart.

Contents

Introduction

꧁꙰꙰꙰꙰꙰꙰꙰꙰꙰꙰꙰꙰꙰꧂

Adult children caring for aging parents can't always find the time to attend a support group or spend hours researching caregiving basics, mental and emotional challenges, and all the necessary information needed to care for their parents. Instead, they need accessible information at their fingertips, quick ideas to solve problems, affirmations to uplift their spirits, and the permission to experience their own feelings.

This book provides useful interventions to reduce family stress and help manage the emotionally difficult situations caregivers face as they tend to elders who eventually decline and need greater assistance. The language used for documents, services, and medical interventions can be confusing, and thus we have provided a Glossary and Resources page at the back of the book. You might want to glance at these pages before you start exploring this guidebook.

Part One

Caregiving Basics

CHAPTER ONE

Beginning Conversations with Your Parents

A conversation about the what-ifs that come with a longer life is fraught with emotions about life and death, family, and change. Adult children often struggle to initiate this critical first step when caring for their aging parent. It's rarely an easy conversation.

Yet it must be addressed.

Adult children need to understand everything—their parents' moral and religious beliefs, their legal rights, their financial situation, and their long-term care desires. Learning how to frame and begin this conversation will keep the dialogue fluid as individual needs and circumstances change.

The approach you take with your parents when discussing changes will be vital to making your conversation with them successful. Careful thought and planning are essential.

A series of short conversations will prevent overwhelming your parent and causing them to resist all suggestions. The exception to this is if someone is a danger to themselves or others.

Tips for Planning Your Conversations

- Plan your approach by first considering your parents' style, values, decision-making skills, history of taking advice, and potential fear of change.

- If your siblings are going to participate in the conversation, have a meeting or phone conference in advance to cover the primary issues and goals. Counsel everyone involved to start all discussions with "I am concerned about…" and avoid "You should . . ." statements.

- Look at the list of important questions and issues to discuss at the end of this chapter and create your own list of necessary documents, contact information, appointments, medications, etc.

- With everyone on the same page and your list completed, talk to your parent about your observations and concerns—and those of others familiar with your elder—making all comments specific to your family's unique situation.

- If you have an overwhelming number of subjects to cover, break them down to more than one session. Try to cover the most pressing or concerning areas at the first meeting. The meeting should not be over one and a half hours.

Sample Script

"Mom/Dad, I/we respect your autonomy and dignity, but we're concerned that if there's a medical crisis or other unknown change we won't know how to assist you. Can we discuss some of the what-ifs of a longer life so we know your desires and wishes, as well as some information about insurance, finances, and long-term care plans like advance directives and other legal issues?"

Key Discussion Points

First, reassure your parent that you respect their ability to manage their affairs without outside help. However, you'll need their input on some universal aging issues so that if they do become dependent, you can make decisions based on their desires and wishes whenever possible and not on the desires and wishes of family members or medical providers.

Second, depending on their response, you might proceed to your list of questions or set up another time to talk. Be prepared to stop at any time, but also don't be surprised if your parent actually welcomes this conversation. It's possible they have been anxious about these issues, but haven't wanted to worry their busy adult children.

The Most Important Issues to Discuss

The following important questions and issues may need to be covered over a series of conversations:

1. Ask them for a list of all insurance carriers and copies of insurance cards.

   a. Request their Medicare number and ask about whether they have Medicare Part D, medigap co-insurance, long-term care insurance, VA benefits, homeowners' insurance, and life insurance policies.

   b. Where are all these policies kept?

2. Ask them for doctors' names and contact information.

   a. What condition(s) is each doctor treating?

   b. What are your parents' current medications?

   c. What is the name/location of their pharmacy?

3. Ask what types of legal documents they have currently drawn up.

   a. Where are these documents kept?

   b. Does your parent know what an advance directive is? Has someone been appointed to make decisions if something were to happen to either of them?

   c. Find out the name and contact information of your parents' attorney, if applicable.

4. Ask if they currently have enough income to cover their expenses.

   a. What is their monthly income and where does it come from?

   b. Do they have direct deposit for this income?

   c. What is the name/location of their bank?

5. Ask if they need everyday help with home upkeep and gardening, shopping, bill paying, driving, etc.

6. Ask if they have any concerns about their memory.

    a. Their response may indicate they are unaware of their declining memory, or that they are concerned but don't know what to do.

    b. Reassure them that there are new medications to help with memory loss.

7. Ask if Mom or Dad has an emergency response system (especially important for people living alone).

8. Ask for names and contact information for their friends—how often are they in contact with these friends? How often do they go to clubs, church, or other gatherings?

9. Ask about and observe their alcohol use; discuss safe driving practices.

10. Ask if they think anyone is taking advantage of them, including telemarketers or other business scams. Be aware that seniors are often embarrassed to tell their children they have been scammed.

You may need to do more research on your own and combine it with the information from your parents. Then create a binder that will help them organize their lives and help you easily find important information in the event of an emergency.

Because you may need to change some information over time—like medical providers or medication lists—pick a date such as a birthday month to annually review and update the information.

Your first priority is to address your parents' immediate concerns, even if you feel overwhelmed and think the first step should be a visit to an elder law attorney. If Mom or Dad wants help with the gardening, let that be the first activity you work on.

Affirmation:

"I know that by helping others, I help myself."

CHAPTER TWO

Safety Concerns

Children of aging parents have a host of safety worries that typically
center on falls, driving, nutrition, and elder abuse. You can mitigate
these risks, but there might be times when it may be appropriate to
let your parent take some chances.

For many families, their worst nightmare is that no one hears an aging parent's cries for help if they fall, or are injured during a natural disaster. Emergencies are not entirely preventable, of course, but we can mitigate them with some common-sense adaptations to the home environment, such as installing mobility supports.

Use a birthday month to check that home safety items are up-to-date and functioning well.

Home Safety Checklist

❑ Are all smoke and carbon monoxide detectors working, and new batteries installed every six months?

❑ An emergency kit at the ready with the following items:

- A three-day supply of food.

- A three-day supply of medications and a complete list of what your parent currently takes.

- Reminder: every time a medication changes, this list must change as well.

❑ A backpack—stored in the closet closest to the front door—containing a spare pair of glasses, underwear, socks, and toiletries, as well as the medications and a list that includes the names of their physicians.

❑ List of emergency numbers (fire, police, or neighbors) near all phones.

❑ If your parents live in areas prone to hurricanes, tornadoes, earthquakes, and fires, have an evacuation plan or a protective area within the home.

Consider bringing in a professional—a nurse or care manager—to tour the home and assess safety. When your parent uses furniture for balance or doesn't keep floors and walkways free of clutter, those are your alerts to bring someone in.

Technological Help in the Home

Improved technology in the home can help give your family peace of mind and significantly extends a parent's ability to remain independent (even if they're resistant to it at first).

For example, Emergency Response Systems are very effective and relatively inexpensive. The monthly fee depends on whether the system has fall detection and/or the ability to call for help in an emergency. Some newer models even have GPS. For those who live alone or are the primary caregiver for someone with impaired memory or judgment, these systems are not only helpful, they're necessary.

In addition, wireless home monitors track your parent electronically in real time. They keep you aware if someone has been to the kitchen, bathroom, or out of the house, and alert you to limited movements or frequent movements—both of which could be a sign that help is needed.

The following reliable sources track the latest technological developments that could help your parent (see the Resources page):

- LeadingAge

- AARP

- Alzheimer's Association

- Age in Place

- Your local care manager or senior information office

Home Remodeling with Universal Design

If you have the resources to remodel your parents' home, consider a universal design layout. Many contractors who specialize in universal design help homeowners remodel or retrofit buildings, so they are more accessible to older people and people with disabilities. Common features of universal design include:

- Doorways wide enough for wheelchairs

- Ramps designed for ease of access

- Bathrooms large enough to accommodate walkers and wheelchairs

- No raised thresholds in the home (including entry doorways)

- Curb-less showers with grab bars

- Door handles are levers instead of round knobs

- Cabinet pulls for ease of use

- Stairlifts

- Railings in long hallways and along stairs

For smaller projects—like installing a new faucet or fitting a ready-made ramp to the front doorway—local volunteer groups will often do handyman work for seniors at no cost.

Other Safety Considerations

Even if a parent is not cognitively impaired, they may not recognize when their home is no longer safe, and sometimes accidents occur before you can make necessary changes. Try to avoid that scenario by sharing your concerns as a family with your parent, and then ask if they would like help finding appropriate safety solutions.

When a parent's health status declines, their physician can order a visit from an occupational therapist, which Medicare home health services may cover. Occupational therapists can introduce the latest technology to help make your parent's home safe and devise creative solutions for everyday problems.

If your parent is living in an unsafe situation, you can call your local elder abuse line. Ask for a health and safety evaluation from their professionals, which may lead to necessary interventions.

Sample Script

"I know you want to stay in your own home for as long as you live. There are some small things we can do to prevent you from having an accident such as breaking a hip and needing long-term care."

Key Discussion Points

- Be prepared to demonstrate that the costs of taking safety precautions are far less than the cost of hospitalization and long-term care.

- Talk about your own emergency plan and ask if you can fill a backpack together (or give a stocked pack to your parent for their birthday or other holiday).

- If there is a change in a parent's status or diagnosis, discuss the benefit of getting a Medicare-covered evaluation that could uncover any mobility or safety issues in the home. Most people appreciate this service, which is usually free or covered under Medicare.

To help avert resistance and resentment, patiently talk about safety concerns every time you visit. Even if you have to make the same suggestions ten times before your parent says yes—don't give up.

Affirmation:

"Safety first gives me peace of mind."

CHAPTER THREE

Understanding Types of Elder Abuse

Unfortunately, physical and emotional abuse of elders happens, often at the hands of family members. It could be due to burnout, over-caring, or the self-interest of the adult child. This abuse causes enormous pain and needs to be confronted honestly and legally. You can learn to identify abuse and use proven methods to prevent it.

Awareness of Elder Abuse

The term "elder abuse" covers many circumstances in which someone causes an elderly person's physical or mental suffering or allows it to happen by putting their health or financial resources in jeopardy.

One in nine seniors suffer abuse in some way, and one out of twenty seniors suffer financial abuse. According to the National Adult Protective Services Association, almost 90 percent of elder abuse involves a family member or other trusted adult.

Education and awareness are key to preventing elder abuse. California Advocates for Nursing Home Reform defines the following multiple types:

- **Abandonment**—the desertion of an elder by a caregiver

- **Abduction**—the removal of an elder to an undisclosed location, without the knowledge or consent of the individual, conservator, or guardian

- **Financial abuse**—the illegal or unethical exploitation or use of an elder's funds, property, or other assets

- **Isolation**—intentionally preventing an elder from receiving mail, telephone calls, or visitors

- **Mental suffering**—the infliction of fear, agitation, or confusion through threats, harassment, or other forms of intimidating behavior

- **Neglect**—the failure to fulfill a caretaking obligation such as assisting in personal hygiene, providing food, clothing, or shelter, or failure to protect an elder from health and safety hazards or prevent malnutrition

- **Physical abuse**—the infliction of physical pain or injury, sexual assault, or the use of physical or chemical restraints—without a doctor's order—as punishment

Ways for Caregivers to Recognize Abuse

Pay attention to observable physical signs. Unexplained weight loss, bedsores, pain when touched, and broken bones can all be signs of both physical abuse and neglect. Note changes in behavior—agitation, anxiety, confusion, helplessness, depression, and/or withdrawal.

Parents can also sometimes suffer financial abuse. Caregivers need to be aware of this kind of abuse and can help their parents who are often specifically targeted.

Share the following tips with your parents, and keep your eyes open for any signs that they are being taken advantage of:

- Never share personal information over the phone. If a bank or financial institution calls and asks for any information, do not give it. Call the phone number on your bank statement or on the back of your credit card to confirm the call was legitimate.

- If you receive an email from a bank, a business, or an other institution—even if you have an account with them—do not open any link or attachment in an email or call any number listed. Find a phone number from a statement and call that number to verify legitimacy.

- Use direct deposit for all regular income.

- Shred personal information before putting it in the trash.

- Do not give home care workers or housekeepers access to your financial information. Do not ask them to do banking for you.

- Check your credit card charges daily or a few times a week. If a credit card is compromised, quickly call the bank and/or close the account.

- Be careful with passwords. Don't use a simple password for everything. Be sure to change passwords a few times a year. Show your parent how to store passwords safely.

- Consult with your attorney or financial planner before loaning money to family members.

- Get home repair estimates in writing. Check to see if the person is a licensed contractor. Pay the balance due only when the job is done to your satisfaction. A licensed contractor can only charge a deposit: $1,000 or 10% of the total cost, whichever is less.

- Never send money in advance to claim a prize. These requests are scams.

- When hiring a caregiver, avoid Craigslist. A referral from a friend or family member of someone experienced may be fine. However, always perform a criminal background check. If hiring from a reputable agency, ask about liability insurance.

- Never allow anyone into your home who claims to be from a utility company and requests to check an appliance or the water.

- Keep valuables in locked drawers or safes. Keep purses and wallets out of sight.

Caregiver Neglect and Self-Neglect

Caregivers—whether hired or family—are legally responsible for ensuring their clients get the care they need, especially clients who suffer from illness or dementia.

Self-neglect is prevalent in elders with dementia and/or who live alone. They may endanger themselves by not properly taking care of their personal hygiene, nutrition, or safety.

When signs of neglect or self-neglect are present, contact your local Adult Protective Services (APS) for help with an intervention.

Affirmation:

"I stay informed as a caregiver and remain alert for information that keeps me and my loved ones safe."

CHAPTER FOUR

Money Management

Due to modern medicine and healthier lifestyles, many people are living far longer than they imagined. The bad news is that many people have not made appropriate financial plans and find their savings depleted far too soon. While you are not legally obligated to take financial responsibility for a parent, you may end up having to. Before taking any action, adult children need to fully understand the resources to which their parent is entitled. If the adult child takes over inappropriately, their parent could lose those benefits.

Adult children who don't have a clear picture of their parents' finances often find Mom or Dad reluctant to share information— either because they are embarrassed to tell their children they don't have enough to meet their expenses, or simply because they don't want to burden their children with money worries.

Learning how to broach the delicate subject that money matters always are, and when to step in, will help you protect your parents from the many scams aimed at taking away their life savings.

Safely Managing Your Parents' Resources

As your parent ages, be aware of the following red flags that may include:

- Unopened mail (some of it looking suspiciously like bills or checks)

- Late payment notices (often pink) that include threats to turn off utilities

- Overpaid bills—especially insurances or taxes—that can indicate your parent has paid the same bill twice

- Changes in the way your parent has traditionally managed his or her money, such as reverting to paying bills in cash

- Not balancing their checkbook

- Frequent references that involve going to the bank

- Excessive concern with every piece of mail from financial institutions

- Changes in your parent's usual gifting pattern, such as a family member receiving a larger or much smaller gift than usual

- Stories about all the contests your parent is on the verge of winning

- Providing information over the phone or internet without knowing who is asking for it (classic behavior for older people who are vulnerable to these types of scams)

- Sudden fear of spending that starts behavior such as cutting medications in half to save money, not heating or cooling their homes, and switching to inexpensive frozen meals

(especially worrisome if your parent has the assets to afford
a healthier lifestyle)

WHEN AND HOW TO INTERVENE ON MONEY MATTERS

Any one of these red flags can be a cue to take action, but this is a
difficult step for both a parent and the adult child.

Plan the conversation carefully to respect your parents' dignity and self-esteem, while also protecting their assets. If you need
outside help, experienced professionals including geriatric care managers can help families manage financial transitions.

Begin your conversation about money with a series of simple
questions:

- Do you feel that you have all the financial resources
  you need?

- Do you have a financial planner?

- Would you share with me where your income comes from
  and where you keep your assets?

- Have you given a durable power of attorney or named
  someone to be your successor trustee in case you have an
  accident or illness and can't manage your money?

- Can I know where these important documents are or have
  a copy of them?

If your parent is already talking to you about their money concerns,
these questions open the door to a simpler, more direct discussion.

Sample Script

"Mom/Dad, would you like me to take over paying all your bills? If you like, we can set up some bills on auto-pay. Your bills will be automatically deducted from your account, so you don't have to worry about them. We can also help with your complicated taxes, so we can collect all the necessary information for any refunds you are due."

If your parent denies having a problem, it will take some tact to create a system that respects their autonomy but protects their assets. You can use "taxes are complicated" to suggest they begin using either an accountant or an other credentialed professional who can also uncover all the benefits your parent is entitled to.

Finally, if your parent has already been scammed, or does not have the mental capacity to manage their finances, consider hiring an elder law attorney to assist you.

Ensuring They Have the Necessary Financial Resources

To get all the benefits your parent is entitled to and help plan for their future care, you need to know where they get their money and any other resources they might have.

Help your parents gather the following financial information:

- Social Security benefits—How much are the benefits? Where is it deposited?

- Retirement income from a former job or a spouse's former job—How much do they receive each month? What is the contact information for this retirement income? Is there a spousal benefit when one of them dies?

- IRA, 401(k), or other retirement savings accounts—What is the account's value? Is your parent withdrawing as specified by the plan or the IRS?

- Securities of any kind—Are the securities with one company or several?

- What is the value? Do they take an income from those funds?

- Current employment income if applicable

- Financial planner and/or stockbroker contact information

For some families, this is a lot to discuss. A parent is often hesitant to share this information—either because they consider it private, or because they are concerned their savings will be stolen. In some cases, they may already have dementia and honestly can't remember where their assets are.

If you find your parent is resistant to sharing this information, ask if they would share it with their attorney. It's not unusual for a resistant parent to trust an attorney or bank trust department over a family member. These professionals tend to be careful and conservative, and typically provide excellent guidance.

Explain how their attorney could arrange for a professional—like a trusted private fiduciary—or a family member to use the funds only according to your parent's desires, should they have a medical issue in the future.

MAKING SMART FINANCIAL DECISIONS

If your parent confides in you and you understand their monthly income and assets, you may need legal documents to assist and protect them. This is especially the case if there are considerable resources.

If, however, your parent only has a limited monthly income, you can look for other support. Because the application process for public benefits is time-consuming and stressful, thoroughly research your parent's assets before applying. For example, you wouldn't want to go through the application only to find out there is stock in your parent's name that disqualifies them from the benefit.

One useful resource is the benefits checkup page on the National Council on Aging's website. You will need to enter a lot of secure information, but it will tell you exactly which national benefits (VA payments, Medicaid, etc.) your parent might qualify for.

Carefully calculate whether your parent has the resources to pay for a serious, long-term illness. Many people are unaware that Medicare does not pay for any long-term care, except on a very limited basis after an illness or accident. If your parent does not have long-term care insurance (or even if they do), you need to determine which services your family member can afford to cover.

It's worth knowing that nearly all communities have resources that could benefit a parent in their own home or in assisted living. To identify these resources, consider consulting a care manager.

Money can be a touchy subject. Tread slowly. If you do take over your parents' finances, don't mingle their funds with yours. You will need to be entirely transparent for other family members and to preserve the possibility of public benefits in the future. If possible, consult with an elder law attorney early in this process for assistance with planning for long-term care.

Affirmation:

"I have the skills and knowledge I need
to care for others and myself."

CHAPTER FIVE

Navigating Legal Issues

Proactive legal planning is recommended for all of us, but especially for those in the winter of their lives. For obvious reasons, legal planning can be a touchy subject. Before talking about the legal tools necessary to manage the financial, medical, and end-of-life affairs of an aging parent, there are concrete steps you can take to make this critical conversation easier.

Legal Tools to Protect and Direct

Unfortunately, people—including family members—have taken advantage of older adults, so a number of laws have been put in place to protect elder rights. Making sure your parent has all the proper legal protections in place and that you are not inadvertently violating their rights requires some research and further discussion.

One helpful way to begin conversation on legal concerns is to speak generally about your own legal tools and how important they are, especially in terms of respecting your wishes around health and medical care. If appropriate, share a story about someone who was ill and didn't have legal tools in place. Emphasize how things didn't play out the way they wanted.

Then ask if your parent has a durable power of attorney (DPOA) for health care, a living trust, and/or other legal directives. If you have a disabled sibling that your parent still cares for, you need to know the long-term plans for them as well.

Legal Guidance for Health Care Decisions

Most experts believe each of us should have a medical advocate to protect our wishes if we are not able to speak for ourselves. This person is typically named in a power of attorney for medical decisions or advance health care directive, both of which are usually standard forms.

In most states, these documents just need to be witnessed, not notarized, unless the person resides in a skilled nursing facility. In that case, most states require an ombudsman to witness the signing.

Typically, you can download the appropriate forms for your state online. Many hospitals have them as well.

HIPAA (Health Insurance Portability and Accountability Act) laws protect our privacy. If a parent becomes incapacitated, the power of attorney for medical decisions or advance health care directive forms allows the person listed (the advocate) to have access to medical providers and medical information. Be sure these documents also have provisions that allow the advocate to get medical information even before your family member is incapacitated.

Many states also honor other forms—such as Five Wishes from the nonprofit organization Aging with Dignity and Prepare for Your

Care from the University of California UC Regents—that give more detailed information about health care and end-of-life decisions (find these under Resources).

An attorney can also customize a durable power of attorney for health care (or an advance health care directive) based on your parent's wishes and according to the laws of that state.

Laws vary by state, but the DPOA for health care or advance health care directive is often the only valid document to arrange a cremation.

A more recent legal tool is the Physician Orders for Life-Sustaining Treatment (POLST), which you or your parent complete and have signed by a physician. It is not currently available everywhere and the options it covers can vary by state. See what your state offers at POLST.org. In California, for example, it must be printed on fluorescent pink paper and allows you to choose from three options: all treatment, limited treatment, or no life-sustaining actions/treatments.

For people with strong feelings about any of these options, this is an important document. In some states, it is the only document emergency responders will read in a real emergency; they will not read the advance health care directive.

Legal Trusts

There are many different kinds of trusts, but individuals with real property use trusts to save on taxes and ease the settling of their estates after death. Trusts also state people's wishes based on their values and desires if they become incapacitated and can't manage their financial or personal affairs. To create a trust, work with an expert in elder or estate-planning law.

A durable power of attorney for finances is often created at the same time as a trust. Your parent names a person who, under certain conditions, will manage assets that are not in the name of the trust. The attorney who produces the trust can also discuss a DPOA for finances with you.

Legal Questions to Ask

If your parent is receptive to a conversation about their legal rights and protections as they age, here are some key questions to ask:

- Do you have a living trust and who is the trustee?
  - o If your parents are very elderly and both are still alive, ask if one is named as agent or trustee. Would one of them be capable of taking over estate management?
  - o Because either parent may become incapable, it is a good idea to have a third person of a younger generation named in these documents.
- Have you transferred all your real property and large bank accounts into the trust's name?
- Where do you keep these documents in case of an emergency?

If your parents resist talking about their legal affairs with you, bring in a professional to talk about all the options to ensure your parents' preferences are respected. That professional can be a care manager, an attorney, or a social worker at a local senior center or hospital.

Affirmation:

"I am grateful and generous with
my time and talents."

CHAPTER SIX

Encountering Resistance

An aging parent's resistance to the changing nature of their
relationship with their child is one of the most common
stumbling blocks in the early stages of the caregiver relationship.
Simple, practical suggestions are often rebuffed. Your parent
may fear loss of control and actively resist your suggestions, even
when they know something needs to change.

Sometimes, such resistance is a symptom of dementia or
related conditions. Other times it may have emerged more recently,
a product of the aging process. And sometimes it is a lifelong
behavior, now exaggerated as your parent ages.

Knowing how to bring resistant behavior to the attention of medical
providers (who can either diagnose or rule out dementia), how to
make suggestions in a gentle, less threatening manner if dementia is
ruled out, and how to pick the right family member to address the
issue at hand will help you remain patient while your parent comes
to terms with the actions or changes they are facing.

When Parents Resist All Your Suggestions

Resistance seems like a "no-win" roadblock to providing support or care. Understanding why older adults resist your suggestions is one key to removing that obstacle.

Patience and preparedness are your best tools to avoid resistance. Try to understand the resistance from your parents' perspective— empathize and listen to their feelings. Address the emotions, not the reality. For example, Mom might resist having "Meals on Wheels" delivered because she can't eat it all; maybe she feels shame for wasting food. Once you address the real issue, give her creative solutions like saving the leftovers for the next meal or sharing them with a friend.

Try not to overcontrol. Humans have a deep need for control; we will first resist anything that looks like it is taking control away from us. Being bossy and saying, "You should" to Mom or Dad will get you a string of nos, even when they might like what you are saying. Introduce ideas without over-managing the outcome. For example, Dad has had some major falls and you want him to try the balance class for seniors at the local physical therapy center. Even though you know this could be the perfect answer, go slow. First find out the cost of the class and if it is covered by insurance. When you know Dad can afford it, perhaps drop off a flyer and ask him to give them a call. This puts the control back in his hands. Don't push. If he doesn't move, gently tell him you know someone who took classes at that center, and they really improved.

Be creative as you introduce new ideas about caregiving, especially if you feel (or the doctor is saying) it is time to bring in a caregiver. But the term "caregiver" often conjures up feelings of being "less than," "helpless," or "weak"—all terms that can cause a parent's immediate reaction, "I am not like that," and then they say no. Parents are often more receptive when you call the caregiver a "personal assistant," "personal trainer," or "cook" because it feels more like a physician's prescription. You are still calling an eldercare agency and asking for a caregiver, but the term you use for this person's role is something your parent agreed to.

Always give choices. If your parent is a risk to others and him/herself, then you need to come in with "tough love." Offer choices, but not the choice to stay in a place where they risk injury to themselves or others. Even though we have a right to risk in our country, if your parent's resistance is the result of dementia, you have to deal with it differently from resistance in mentally alert elders. It becomes your responsibility to secure your parent's safety and well-being.

For example: Mom, you require this "X" (senior housing or home care) because the doctor says it is necessary. We have two choices: either bring in a "housekeeper" who is really a trained caregiver from an agency, or we try the "senior community" (hopefully you can name one where Mom might know someone).

If their response to planning for the future is "I am not ready yet," and they still have not completed legal documents, you truly need to get creative about assisting them. Help your parent understand that by working with you and thinking through their future, they will have more control if they are ill or lose capacity in the short term or longer term. Taking your resistant parent to a lecture on planning for the "what-ifs of a longer life" is often the best trick. But sometimes parents still see you as a child. Bringing in care managers or aging life care experts to start the conversation makes any decisions about resources one your parent made with a professional instead of with their child. Find information on locating an Aging Life Care Professional* in the Resources section.

If your elder is not a risk to self or others, then patience is the key. If you can, find a support group for yourself. A sounding board is helpful in these challenging times; talking about your experience helps lower stress and find new solutions from others going through the same issues.

The resistance from elders with early dementia—sometimes called MCI (mild cognitive impairment)—can be the most challenging because making decisions can be very hard for them.

An excellent way to approach any suggestion is to call it a "trial period." Try the senior center meals or the personal trainer or the assisted living for two months. This gives them an out and most people, after two months, adjust nicely to new ideas. Try not to promise what is not possible, but you can emphasize that the change is likely only temporary by assuring them, "Just until the doctor says you can return to your old lifestyle."

Sample Script:

"I know you want to go home, Mom, but your doctor has not released you (or give a concrete example like 'but the plumbing is not repaired'). *Let's go look at the bird bath/fish tank* (or whatever is pleasing in the new environment)."

Distraction and assisting in building new relationships will be your tools. Introduce your parent to another resident in an activity and get them talking, then step back.

Affirmation:

"I am patient; being so keeps me calm."

CHAPTER SEVEN

Setting Limits

While many aging parents fear loss of control and resist help,
they may at the same time demand an enormous amount
of emotional, social, and logistical support. They may make
comments such as "I don't know what I would do if I didn't
have you," or "How can you leave me with a stranger?" Your
parent may make impossible-to-keep promises about a future
that cannot be foreseen, especially given the realities of changing
medical needs and financial concerns.

Yet for the adult child, saying "No" or setting limits on
an ill, confused, or frail parent can foster enormous guilt and
sadness. And too often, one family caregiver shoulders what
becomes an unfair burden.

Setting limits and finding balance helps avoid burnout
in your caregiving journey.

Setting Limits (How to Say "No")

When your older parent is ill or has limited outside contact, they can become very demanding of your attention, especially if you are the primary person to give or oversee care.

At first, the demands—like food, bathroom assistance, or picking up something—can seem valid, even if you have already set up systems to support their independence.

But when the demands become overwhelmingly frequent or inappropriate, many people struggle to set limits. After all, saying, "No" or "Just a minute" to someone with a serious deficit can seem cruel. Nevertheless, if you don't learn how to identify and stick with important limits, you are not only making your own life impossible, but could harm your parent by giving them a false sense of security that you will be there 24/7.

Recognizing the Patterns and Understanding the Reasons

As with so many solutions, the first step in setting limits is to recognize the demand patterns then assess what drives them.

One pattern we frequently see is an older parent calling their adult child at an inappropriate time for a quart of milk or some fresh fruit—even though the child was already planning to shop for food the next day. Failing to say "No" in this instance likely means you will arrive with the milk, angry and resentful. In turn, your parent will become defensive and the situation will deteriorate because no one is talking about the real issue: Either your parent is lonely and craves personal interaction, or you are witnessing the onset of dementia.

Help set realistic limits and manage expectations—while incorporating your understanding of your parent's situation—using the following steps:

1. Have your parent keep a running list of things they need and tell them exactly when you will be doing the shopping or errands, and then stick to that plan.

2. For the occasional urgent errand, have a next-door neighbor, friend, or caregiving agency on call to run the errand.

3. If the pattern continues, consider senior services such as peer counselors or a Stephen Minister from a local church. These are people trained to visit with a purpose and can make a big difference in reducing unrealistic calls or demands.

Of course, setting limits is rarely easy; it is fraught with the potential for guilty feelings on your part and resentment from your parent. It's important to remember the things you are already doing—including setting up a backup plan for real emergencies and arranging for community visitors.

Again, it helps to attend a good support group or talk with a friend to gain perspective. Because even love, after all, has its limits.

Affirmation:

"I keep a healthy balance between responsibilities and relationships."

CHAPTER EIGHT

Sharing the Caregiving Load

In the United States, about 80 percent of all caregiving is provided by family members. Family caregiving often imposes an enormous toll on marriages, careers, personal interests, and health—in short, on every aspect of one's life. If the caregiving burden is not monitored and shared, it can negatively affect the health of the sole care provider, much to the detriment of the older family member.

The sole care provider needs to take care of themselves by sharing the caregiving duties. A common solution is to either pay family members from the elder's estate, or to provide respite for the person contributing the lion's share of the care duties.

Avoiding Caregiving Burnout

Burnout occurs because caregiving is a 24/7 responsibility. This doesn't mean caregiving can't be rewarding; after all, it is very much an act of love and appreciation. Yet, if you are not rested or don't have other interests and relationships to bring balance to your life, you are almost certainly short-changing not just yourself, but the person you care for.

The following tips may help a caregiver prevent burnout:

- Have a care partner from the beginning who can be another family member, a friend, or a paid in-home care companion. Allow this person to be Mom or Dad's caller or visitor at least one day every week.

- Regularly tell someone in your circle of friends and family how you are balancing caregiving duties for your parent with other activities.

- Feed your soul with physical activity and creative pursuits. Take time to read a good book, take a walk, or have a nice dinner.

- Focus on your health. Eat a heart-healthy diet and exercise daily. Try to practice some form of mindfulness every day: a walk, prayer, yoga, meditation, focused breathing, or anything that slows you down and allows you to be aware of how you live your life.

- Ask for help in ways that are clear to others. Rather than saying, "I need help," be specific.

Sample Script

"I need some support caring for Mom. Can you take her to her weekly doctor's appointment?"

Consider a Caregiver Contract

Sometimes one child in a family retires early to care for a parent, which can negatively impact the child's savings and retirement funding. In order to help the family caregiver, many families design a way to pay the caregiver from the elder's estate.

To help you and your family avoid any misunderstandings, find an elder law attorney to help create a contract *before* the caregiving arrangement begins. The contract should clearly state the caregiver's duties, schedule, respite (time off, including vacation), and wage. It is crucial that everyone in the family understands and signs off on the agreement.

Affirmation:

"I take care of my emotional health
with mini-retreats of time alone."

CHAPTER NINE

Consulting Caregiving Professionals

Four types of professionals can guide families through the caregiving process: geriatric care managers, elder law attorneys, financial planners, and certified public accountants. Consulting these professionals can bring you both peace of mind and protection from scams aiming to take advantage of your aging parents.

Defining Different Caregiving Professionals

If you try to take caregiving tasks alone, caring for an elder who has lost capacity due to dementia or physical frailty is often an overwhelming responsibility. Most of us are not prepared to be doctor, nurse, attorney, financial expert, and caregiving expert rolled into one. Even if we wear one of those hats in our professional career, it is challenging to be objective with our own family member. Yet, all these important roles help maintain an elder's well-being and long-term care.

Having a trusted professional team is often the best way to ensure the highest possible quality of life for your parent. It can also save considerable time and money.

Whether you can afford to hire the best experts available or need to rely on public services and nonprofit organizations, using the four professionals mentioned below can help you and your loved one plan for the best life possible.

PROFESSIONAL GERIATRIC CARE MANAGER

First, start by contacting a geriatric care manager. Hospitals or medical organizations use the term "care manager" for a variety of services. But the professional geriatric care manager or an Aging Life Care Professional* does not usually deal directly with medical issues but advocates and supports the plans of medical providers. They make sure that medical care is only handled by medical professionals and can arrange for second opinions or find physicians trained in geriatric medicine or psychiatry.

A professional geriatric care manager usually has an advanced degree and certifications. They understand the technologies, benefits, entitlements, housing, options, aging, illnesses, and strategies for dementia behavior and family conflicts. They also follow a code of ethics and standard of practice to ensure your parent's best quality of life.

Geriatric care managers/aging life care experts help with the following:

- Assess your parent's needs, provide a roadmap for now and the future, and find local organizations or professionals to consult

- Offer behavioral interventions for dementia and often provide 24/7 coaching for families with dementia challenges

- Assist with placement, moving, medical advocacy, family conflict, benefits, and caregiving oversight

- Provide an assessment to give attorneys, financial planners, and other professionals who need to understand your parent's values, preferred options, and financial resources

- Refer you to professionals who specialize in your specific concern or need

- Oversee home care plans and become the conduit to family and medical professionals in the coordination of ongoing plans of care in the home or a community care facility

ELDER LAW ATTORNEY

Laws frequently change, so to avoid needless taxes or complications, you must continually update a living trust that was created earlier. Even if you have health and financial documents in place, checking with an elder law attorney can save you a major headache or legal battle down the road.

An elder law attorney can help with the following:

- Secure government benefits earlier than you assumed (a serious consideration should one or both of your parents need skilled and expensive care)

- Design your parents' trust to meet their values and wishes

- Draft end-of-life documents specific to each of your parents' desires, with all the information necessary for making challenging medical decisions

CERTIFIED FINANCIAL PLANNER (CFP)

Wise investing with a certified financial planner helps you arrange for in-home care or retirement living—both of which are typically quite expensive. Even if you already have a CFP, consider getting a second opinion by one who doesn't work on commission but only advises and manages investments. Ask your elder law attorney or professional geriatric care manager/Aging Life Care Professional* to recommend a certified financial planner.

CERTIFIED PUBLIC ACCOUNTANT (CPA)

Managing a beloved elder's daily spending, taxes, or decisions about selling property can be an enormous emotional burden that can also cause a considerable dent in family finances. Ask an elder law attorney or CFP for a referral to a competent CPA—one who specializes in helping older adults and their families understand the tax consequences of bad or premature moves in property, cash, or securities management.

These professionals can also protect you from being charged with exerting undue influence on your parent, especially if you are the trustee or hold durable power of attorney for health care and/or finances.

Affirmation:

"I have peace of mind because I have a team of experts guiding and coaching me to create the highest quality of life possible for my parent."

Part Two

Helping Your Parent Cope with Declining Health

CHAPTER TEN

Health and Family

The decline of a parent almost always results in grief for the adult child—a grief that can immobilize you. It can be difficult to make the necessary changes a parent's health and well-being now demands.

Part Two of this book focuses specifically on health issues.

Maintaining your partnership with an aging family member requires facing the realities of their changing health. Learning to separate normal aging from the signs and symptoms of Mom or Dad's underlying illness often comes from interacting with the medical community and addressing your concerns.

Concerns about the health of your aging family member range from getting a good diagnosis to medication management. But when family members disagree about treatment options or approaches, managing an elder's health becomes especially challenging.

The first step in overcoming these challenges is to be realistic about what can be done. Adult children can instinctively deny the full truth of their parent's declining health, then become immobilized by it. While finding the right doctor and seeking second opinions is important, it's also important not to fall into a pattern of running from doctor to doctor looking for the answer you want to hear, rather than the truth.

Normal aging differs for everyone, but it almost always means changes in stamina, energy, the musculoskeletal system, and bodily functions like sight, hearing, and taste.

Signs and symptoms that can signal a serious medical event include the following:

- Loss of consciousness (even for a few seconds)
- Loss of ability to walk, talk, or respond
- Any sudden change in mental functioning
- Vomiting and/or diarrhea, where the resulting dehydration can cause changes in electrolytes and adversely affect major organs
- Changes in weight (up or down) in a short period of time
- Sudden inability to find words (not part of aging or dementia)
- Sweating and changes in skin tone
- Blood in the stool, or changes in odor or color of urine
- Sudden hair loss
- Change of mood or behaviors (especially when they come on suddenly)

- Other changes that are not part of your parent's normal personality or usual routine

It's a good idea to bring any changes to the attention of a physician, even if you expected those changes or your parent seems normal. Sudden changes can be a symptom of something more serious, and a physician could suggest simple solutions or adaptations.

Make sure your parents have their hearing and vision tested every year. This ensures they have the correct devices (hearing aids, glasses, etc.) they need to avoid compromising their mental and physical health, or quality of life.

Exercise and a healthy lifestyle help reduce or delay normal aging declines. But Mom doesn't have to go to the gym, especially if she has never been big on physical exercise. There are other, simpler ways to make sure she is getting enough movement.

Activities such as yoga, walks in the park, or the local zoo can be fun and not even thought of as exercise. Swimming or water aerobics is gentle and those who were swimmers find it fun. If Mom has dementia, these fun activities could be good outings for caregiver and Mom.

If your family member has trouble with balance or movement in general, a referral to a physical therapist can help. Going to an exercise program at the local senior center or having a personal trainer come to the house helps improve your elder's well-being.

Social isolation is detrimental to health. Be sure your parents are engaged in local activities, or have a paid companion bring activities into their home.

Educate everyone in the family about the conditions your older family member is experiencing. Reliable, informational websites such as the National Institutes of Health, Mayo Clinic, or WebMD can be very helpful. When you find helpful information, perhaps print it out for the whole family.

Sometimes local hospitals offer classes on the conditions your family member is experiencing. This reliable information can make an enormous difference for everyone, and help you prepare for the future.

Keep a current, electronic list of medications that you can easily update and send to other family members or print out for new medical providers. And put an updated, printed version in a hospital-ready folder or plastic sleeve near the door of your elder's home in their emergency backpack.

This list should include the following:

- both the brand and generic names of the medications

- the dose and number of times taken per day

- why it has been prescribed

- instructions for how and when to take each medication

Use reliable websites affiliated with well-known health care institutions (such as the Mayo Clinic) to look up the potential side effects of all new medications.

If your parent is taking more than three or four medications, check with a board-certified geriatric pharmacist to understand how medicines can interact as well as medications that might have adverse effects. If your parent is experiencing side effects to a medication, report it to the prescribing physician.

Having a relationship with your elder's primary care physician is so valuable. Being able to easily communicate with that physician is one reason why you and your family members should sign a HIPAA (confidentiality) release form.

Having your parent sign a HIPAA form at the doctor's office gives that office permission to speak to you about health issues. If you already have a durable power of attorney for health care, you can often sign the document without a parent's signature. Some medical practices or hospital groups have their own process for sharing or not sharing information.

If your family member has dementia or is otherwise impaired, it is good to attend appointments with them. Create a list of questions before your visit. Email your concerns to the physician before the visit, so you are both on the same page.

If, for any reason, you are not comfortable with your family member's physician—and live near an academic medical center—you can often get a second opinion at the center's geriatric clinic. For more information on resources, including support groups and/or classes for family members, contact your local Office on Aging through the Eldercare Locator website.

Affirmation:

"I have done my best and can rest assured that I have planned for any possible emergencies."

CHAPTER ELEVEN

Managing Medications

Adult children of aging parents are often overwhelmed by
the number of medications their parents take and might seek
uninformed second opinions or get information online that could
cause dangerous misuse of their parents' medications.

Adult children need to understand how to manage these
medications and the changes in how they are taken—
particularly after a hospital discharge.

Medication errors happen in all settings, but at home may be the most dangerous place for them.

First, many older adults use a staggering number of medications. Second, family members often struggle to keep track of the current ones. Third, few families have expert medication managers in-house.

In many states, caregivers cannot actually administer medications, but can only remind clients when to take them. Keep an up-to-date list of medications that any physician has approved. The following time-tested tips will help you manage your family member's medications in a chart with the following columns:

- The date your parent began the medication

- Reason for the medication: sometimes a drug is prescribed for an unexpected reason, i.e., an antidepressant prescribed for pain

- Name of the prescribing physician

- Dosage

- Time(s) of day the medication is taken

- Comments containing additional information or instructions, such as when or how a medication needs to be taken

Keep this list in your hospital-ready packet and be sure to update the list every time there is a change.

In the same hospital-ready packet, also keep the following:

- A history of medications that have been discontinued and/ or that have caused adverse or allergic reactions

- A separate list of all over-the-counter medications used and how often they should be used

A list of all vitamins, herbs, and other supplements with their dosage information. *Note: Some supplements can have dangerous interactions with medications, so be sure attending medical providers are aware of these supplements.*

Use only one pharmacy so your pharmacist can stay on top of potential drug interactions. Keep the phone number of that pharmacy near the telephone and on your prescription list.

For managing medications at home, the following tips might help:

- Medication dispensers distribute medications into a cup and even ring a bell to remind patients when it is time to take them. Other technology alerts individuals when to take medication. But especially for patients in the dementia process, some supervision will still be necessary.

- Store all medications in the same place—one that is dark and dry. Inside a cabinet in the kitchen is often good, as long as it isn't over the stove or sink. Humidity affects medications, so don't store them in the bathroom.

Hospital Discharges and Medication Changes

It's not unusual for your family member to be disoriented when they are discharged from the hospital. Before they are discharged, a family member must understand any new medications and can set up the medications as prescribed.

If your parent receives new medications to replace the ones they took before going into the hospital, make sure you know what to do with the old medications. Should you keep them or dispose of them?

Within two weeks after discharge, make an appointment with the family member's primary care physician to go over the changes and talk about any updates. Many hospitals now use hospitalists (inpatient physicians exclusive to hospitals) to oversee inpatient care, which may cause disagreement or communication gaps between the hospitalist and your family member's primary care physician. Be sure to tell both doctors if they advise different things and ask them to come to an expert consensus.

Hiring Help to Manage Medications

You can hire someone to help manage your parent's medications— almost a must if family can't help after a hospitalization. If your parent is on multiple medications, you likely will need a nurse or professional geriatric care manager (if allowed by law). This person makes regular visits (preferably weekly) to set up medications and answer clinical questions.

Affirmation:

"I consult experts when my family member's needs exceed my knowledge and I ask good questions about every treatment."

CHAPTER TWELVE

Medical Appointments and Care Coordination

Juggling appointments and other medical-compliance issues is often a full-time job for adult children of aging parents.

Families can divide the tasks around managing appointments to reduce stress and prevent burnout for any one family member.

Lack of coordination is one of the most common reasons for medical errors—one physician isn't aware of what another physician has diagnosed or prescribed. But it can also happen in families, often because one person fails to communicate clearly about medications or a change in their parent's well-being.

Such errors are rarely intentional, but they are avoidable. Choose a point person (can be a geriatric care manager, family member, or care coordinator) who is responsible for communicating and updating the entire medical team. Whoever takes your parent to a medical appointment automatically and immediately relays the latest information to the point person so everything and everyone is up-to-date.

Be sure to keep records of the following:

- **Doctors and their specialties:** list the primary doctor first then the specialists or occasional doctors. For each one, include their office address, phone number, and days the office is open.

- **Appointments:** keep a list of all past and future appointments. To minimize waiting time, try to make your parent's appointment the first one of the day or the first one after lunch. For each appointment, list both the questions that were covered and the doctor's answers or recommendations, as well as any changes in the treatment plan.

- **Medications:** refer to Chapter 11 for more information about the lists you should keep (current medication, discontinued medication, over-the-counter medication, and vitamins/supplements).

- **Surgeries and Hospitalizations:** list the date and location of each hospitalization, the reason, and the outcome.

- **Family History:** even if your parent doesn't have the same medical conditions as other family members, keeping a list will help you give every medical provider a complete and consistent picture. List all major illnesses and causes of death for parents and siblings, as well as any other information you might have—such as exposure to toxic substances earlier in life.

- **Well-being journal:** this record helps medical providers know when pain or a change in health started and what was going on at the time. Medicine is sometimes like a detective story and the who, what, when, where, why, and how are important for diagnosis and treatment. For example, if your parent starts to complain about a stomachache after breakfast and this is a new symptom, be sure to record it even if the symptom goes away. Include as much information as possible, such as what your parent had for breakfast that day or if anything was causing them anxiety.

- **Physical activities:** list all the exercise—both formal and informal—your parent does and for how long. Even simple exercise for just 30 minutes a day can be enormously important for health and well-being.

There are computer programs that help gather information, but if you prefer handwritten notes, a simple lined notebook works. Either way, taking your parent's complete information to all appointments and making sure the primary care physician is up-to-date can make a big difference.

If you are dividing tasks between siblings, talk about who prefers to make all the phone calls or prefers taking your parent to appointments. Distribute tasks so that it feels fair to everyone and does not cause resentment.

Affirmation:

"I connect to those in need with my
time and resources."

CHAPTER THIRTEEN

Communicating with Physicians

Having a medical team that works well with you and your parent is a crucial part of the caregiving process—but finding the right balance can be a challenge. Privacy laws, your parents' reluctance to have you speak with their doctors, time limitations, and a physician's lack of experience working with a geriatric population can all pose obstacles.

Selecting the right doctor for your parent includes knowing you can communicate well and work together with them.

Older adults often cope with many different conditions and medications, so having a regular primary care or family practice physician is very important for your parent's health. But identifying the right medical provider can be complicated because not all providers accept Medicare, and not all HMOs allow you to go to your favorite doctor.

Ideally, your parent's physician is board-certified in geriatric medicine and has expert understanding of working with people age 65 and older. Geriatric nurse practitioners also receive specialized training for working with older adults. Although some general practitioners understand and have a passion for working with older adults and their families, most have little formal training in geriatric medicine.

Once you have chosen a health care provider, communicating well with them will help maintain a parent's health and dignity. Be sure the provider has a clear record of all the other specialists your parent sees (bring your lists to all appointments). Have your parent sign a medical release for each provider and give each one a copy of your durable power of attorney for health care.

If your parent is experiencing cognitive decline or dementia, send the doctor a list of your concerns before each appointment, which helps avoid any embarrassing exchanges during the actual appointment. Sometimes—especially when there is cognitive decline—a medical provider will address you and ignore your parent. In most cases, your parent will notice. If this happens, you can gently touch your parent and look at them when answering the provider.

Sample Script

While looking at your mom say, *"Mom, I think it was last Monday you started having those stomachaches after eating."*

Hopefully, the provider will get the message that dignity and respect are important—no matter how much dementia or cognitive impairment an individual might have.

Affirmation:

"Love is doing what is needed, not what is necessarily wanted."

CHAPTER FOURTEEN

Preparing for Hospitalizations

For an aging parent, hospitalizations are often traumatic, and can lead to a rapid decline. Even a high-functioning parent can become disoriented and confused during and after a hospitalization.

Many hospitals do not have trained geriatricians on staff. Medical teams may incorrectly assume a patient has permanent dementia, as opposed to the temporary confusion caused by their diagnosis and/or the unfamiliar hospital environment.

If an adult child (or advocate) is not available for questions and consultations, this could start an unnecessary, detrimental chain of events—older adults are often placed in a dementia-focused skilled nursing center or on a psychotropic medication. This leads to follow-up care that permanently locks them into what should have been a temporary condition.

When an aging parent is hospitalized, emotions are heightened. The grief, fear, and denial family members experience can distort planning and the decision-making processes.

Adult children should know about the important safeguards their
parents with dementia need, even if they manage hospitalization
from a distance during this difficult time.

Hospitalization can be traumatic for anyone; it becomes even more so as we age. If hospital staff has no background knowledge for an older patient, they frequently mistake temporary disorientation for permanent dementia and medicate for it. Unfortunately, this mistake can be devastating for aftercare, recovery, and quality of life.

People with dementia are not good historians. The hospital team has little to go on regarding your elder's history of pain, discomfort, or why they're in the hospital now. It is critical for the team to know your family member's medical history and—especially if they really have dementia—that a family member or professional advocate will accompany the elder as much as possible during their stay. It's the best way to ensure appropriate care and recovery.

During admission, the hospital usually won't ask about special health treatments. If your family member has multiple diagnoses and special restrictions—such as diabetic diets—you can and should advocate for continuing your family member's normal health management.

After hospitalization, we often see a rapid decline or major change in a person's ability to live alone or manage their health. Though these changes are upsetting, for some families they also present a window of opportunity to work with the hospital's treatment and discharge teams to make necessary changes.

The following tips can help a parent and caregiver with what to do before, during, and after a hospital stay.

Before a hospital stay becomes necessary, double-check that your hospital-ready packet has current information for the following:

❑ Advance directives (durable power of attorney for health care) and the POLST (Physician Orders for Life-Sustaining Treatment), if you have them; contacts (both family and medical providers)

❑ List of current health conditions and medications containing the condition and dosage information, since many medications are used for treating a variety of medical issues

❑ Any allergies to medications, foods, or environmental irritants, written in bold; special equipment used—from hearing aids to dentures to walkers

❑ If your parent wears eyeglasses, include a pair in this packet so they can read admission forms.

• If you live far away but have legal power to oversee care, fax or email the above documents to the emergency room or admitting floor.

• Ask if your parent is being "admitted" or is on "observation." The latter would not qualify your family member for skilled nursing after-care that is paid by Medicare.

• Make a note on the admission forms of personal, special equipment (from the list above) that your parent uses. If these items are lost during the hospital stay, the hospital will likely replace them, but only if you have listed them as personal and necessary items.

- Ask a friend or contact a professional to be with your family member in the hospital as soon as they're admitted, and to stay with them.

- If your parent has dementia, try to make sure they are placed as close to the nurses' station as possible.

- Ask questions about any new medications or changes in current medications. You are probably the one who knows best if medications have caused adverse reactions. An allergic reaction to a drug should have already been noted in Mom or Dad's medical records.

- Always ask about palliative care (comfort measures, pain reduction). Palliative care does not always mean end-of-life care or hospice, and in most cases it is available for any life-altering condition.

- If surgery is recommended or necessary, ask about the risks and base your decision on your parent's wishes—not everyone wants the most aggressive treatment.

This can be an emotional time for families, and heightened emotions can lead to conflicts about treatments. Seek a social worker or hospital chaplain's assistance to work with your family. Getting support helps make *you* a better advocate for your hospitalized family member's needs.

Affirmation:

"I have the information I need to make good decisions and I know where to find support."

CHAPTER FIFTEEN

Managing the Hospital Discharge

During your elder's discharge from the hospital, it's especially important for family or a caregiver to be with them. The discharge process is fraught with challenges and too often moves in a direction the family doesn't expect.

Having a checklist of questions to ask the hospital or doctor before your parent is discharged helps families know what's changed, what to watch for, and what to do after your family member returns home from any hospitalization. Know which entitlements your parent qualifies for, and for how long.

When the hospital tells you that your parent is ready to be discharged, it's common to feel unprepared. There are many things to consider when helping your parent make a successful transition from hospital to home—one that minimizes the risk of readmission.

A first question is often: "What care will he/she need at home?" Remember that it is okay to ask for help! Trained professionals, such as a discharge planner or transitional care manager, can do everything from ordering necessary equipment to providing a list of home care companies.

Here are our top tips for making the hospital discharge easier:

1. Contact the discharge/transition team when your family member is first admitted and tell them everything you can about your home's condition and your ability to provide support. This helps the discharge team determine if your parent needs transitional time in a skilled nursing/rehabilitation center first. Check with Medicare—your parent may be eligible for Medicare-covered in-home health care.

2. Regardless of your parent's immediate destination, make sure you (or a trusted friend or family member) are with your elder at the moment of discharge. Make sure you understand the diagnosis, the prescribed aftercare, and any changes in medications. Ask if the old medications at home need to be safely destroyed and where to do that. Many communities have places to take outdated and unneeded medications.

3. Ask as many questions as necessary for you to understand what took place in the hospital, and how that changes your parent's lifestyle, diet, and/or medications. Some changes may apply for a short time; others could be more permanent. Be sure to ask for training on any new procedure or equipment.

4. Before your parent is discharged, set a follow-up appointment with their primary care physician and/or any specialists. When you make it, be clear that your family member was just hospitalized, and you need an appointment within the next 7-10 days.

5. Ask about any danger signs to watch for at home and what to do if symptoms develop. In most cases, hospitals will advise you to call 911.

6. Order all new equipment and medications before your parent is discharged. In some cases, you may need to pick up medications on your way home. If oxygen or other medical equipment is necessary, make sure they're in place before your elder returns home. Know who placed the order and how to contact the supplier.

7. It's common for older family members to be weakened—physically or mentally—from their hospital stay. They usually need time to ease back into prior routines, so don't expect your normally spry, active parent to do the laundry. Be ready to give that support or hire an in-home care companion for the first few days.

8. If you are going to hire a home-care aide for the transition, make sure their home health agency has all the discharge instructions. Enlist the help of the agency's nurses or professional geriatric care managers to guarantee the aide is following all the new protocols.

Sample Script:

"Mom has to take her medications with food so we designed an activity booklet for you to record the time and what she ate each time she received her medications." Or: "Dad has to elevate his legs for two hours in the mornings and two hours in the afternoon. Please record this in his activity booklet. If he refuses, call his son Mark."

Being specific and giving follow-up directions is helpful to paid caregivers and can assure a better recovery. Many hospital transitional care managers follow up with phone calls or home visits to see that the necessary changes have been made. But not all hospitals offer this service, so be sure to ask if yours does.

It is important to ask a discharge planner about possible entitlements your family member might qualify for after care, such as Medicare benefits. You'll want to know how long they will receive these services and who pays once the benefit runs out. If your parent is low income and they need skilled nursing because home care is too expensive and their needs are great, they would qualify for Long Term Care Medicaid benefits. It is important that the discharge is to a facility that accepts Medicaid when Medicare ends.

A good resource to see what benefits/entitlements your family might qualify for is on the National Council for Aging's benefits checkup website.

Slow down, breathe, and get the support you need. Going in and out of the hospital is hard on both you and your older family member.

Affirmation:

"I have a plan, I am prepared for the what-ifs, and I don't have to be the only one. I can share the care."

Part Three

A Parent's Mental and Emotional Challenges

CHAPTER SIXTEEN

Identifying a Parent's Depression

Aging brings loss. Much of this loss—changes in physical well-being or the deaths of cherished friends—is natural. Other changes, such as investment losses or cuts in community services, are less expected but can be equally painful. For many aging adults, these losses can cause clinical depression and/or situational depression.

Caregivers often think that withdrawal from activities or weight loss are due to physical challenges or health issues, but depression may be the culprit. The good news is depression is treatable, and treatment can dramatically improve an elder's quality of life.

Knowing the red flags that signal clinical depression helps families recognize when they need a professional evaluation. Learn how to broach the subject of depression with other family members and how to work with medical providers to treat it.

When an older adult suddenly pulls back from social engagements, or seems down or out of sorts, consider the possibility they may be depressed. Clinical depression is a medical diagnosis; families and individuals often make excuses for their behavior (such as blaming the weather or a recent illness or loss) or feel ashamed. Depression can impact everyday functioning, as well as contribute to other negative health issues, so it is important to get an accurate diagnosis. Elders and their caregiving families can benefit from medication and/or counseling, whether they are suffering from clinical depression or not.

For family caregivers who are tired and stressed, it's easy to overlook depression and ignore the red flags. It may seem logical to the caregiver that the elder is merely reacting to a new diagnosis, for instance, instead of being deeply depressed.

According to the National Institute of Mental Health, symptoms of depression may include the following:

- Difficulty concentrating, remembering details, and making decisions

- Fatigue and decreased energy

- Feelings of guilt, worthlessness, and/or helplessness

- Hopelessness and/or pessimism

- Insomnia, early-morning wakefulness, or excessive sleeping

- Irritability, restlessness

- Loss of interest in activities or hobbies once pleasurable, including sex

- Overeating or appetite loss

- Persistent aches or pains, headaches, cramps, or digestive problems that do not ease with treatment

- Persistent sad, anxious, or empty feelings

- Thoughts of suicide or suicidal attempts

For some, depression can be seasonal, especially when the days are shorter and there is less exposure to natural light. If your family member is only depressed during the dark winter months, consider purchasing a sun lamp to use a few times every day. But, always use caution when using any artificial sunlight products to prevent burns or overexposure.

Tips for Approaching Someone You Think Is Depressed:

- Always start with an "I" message, such as "I notice you are not your same old self and you seem sad and aren't enjoying things as much lately." This is typically more effective than saying, "You seem depressed."

- Give examples of people you know who have been treated for depression. For example, "My friend Susan was experiencing some of the same things you are, and her doctor gave her an antidepressant. It took a few weeks, but she's feeling much better; she's like a new person."

- If depression runs in your family, try to share some hope. "I remember when Grandpa was down and stopped coming to family events. What you're experiencing might run in our family. The good news is that nowadays there are new medications that are very effective."

- If your parent doesn't want to take medication (or if their medication seems inappropriate to a physician), talk therapy can often ease a temporary condition. Ask your parent's physician for a referral to a good therapist, who specializes in working with older adults.

- If your family member lives alone or is isolated for any reason, moving to a more social setting could work wonders. It is crucial to tell your parent this move is not forever. You might say, "Maybe we can try the assisted living that your friend moved into, just to try it out and see if that makes a difference." But it is possible that after a few months they may choose this new social setting as a permanent option.

Additionally, many communities have programs to help with socializing. Your local area's Office on Aging might be able to provide local resources, many of which are free. Some communities also offer free, trained peer counselors for people who are only mildly depressed.

While it is important to be sensitive to the feelings of the person who is depressed, there are circumstances in which it is crucial to act quickly and hospitalize someone who is withdrawing, not eating, or moving toward a "failure to thrive" diagnosis.

Affirmation

"I do my best leading my family
to good choices. At times I have
to take action."

CHAPTER SEVENTEEN

Identifying a Parent's Anger

Some parents begin expressing a lot of anger as they age, often due to a combination of grief, depression, and/or despair. Other aging parents may have always been difficult or hard to please. Either way, an aging parent's anger can pose a difficult challenge for a caregiver, but that is especially the case for adult children who may be dealing with patterns that go back to early childhood.

Addressing an angry parent in a non-threatening manner acknowledges the parent's feelings while avoiding arguments and no-win rationalizations. But sometimes it's best to let others take over.

It's quite common for an aging parent to be angry. Anger may be an emotion you have rarely witnessed in your parent previously, and this change may feel frightening and immobilizing. On the other hand, your older parent may have shown anger throughout their life, but that anger may be escalating—partly in response to a loss of independence. In either scenario, dealing with a parent's anger can greatly complicate the already stressful challenge of providing support or care.

Dealing with this anger can be a particular hurdle if your parent was abusive to you when you were younger. If that is the case, this is likely the time to bring in professionals for guidance and direct care.

If you find that every time you leave your parents' home you have a stomachache, headache, or feel like screaming, it is most likely time to bring in support. Sometimes, a partner who has less emotional baggage can be a helpful stand-in, at least as a starting point.

Effectively Using Active Listening

Reasoning or arguing with an angry person can be counterproductive and self-defeating. We often suggest using active listening, which simply means listening and then responding in a way that tells your parent that they've been heard.

For example, despite cooking exactly what she wanted—from her own recipe!—your mom might angrily say, "Everything you cook for me tastes the same. Why can't you give me what I want?"

In this instance, rather than defending yourself, you should let her speak her piece and then respond, "It sounds to me as though you are disappointed with the meal and everything tastes the same to you."

She may not calm down immediately, but knowing she's been heard can help defuse a volatile situation. As a side note, it is *very* common for older adults to lose their sense of taste, which can be a source of great frustration. Try using more spices and making the plates look more appealing with a garnish or extra color.

Perhaps your father—who is the primary caregiver—says, "I don't need any help with your mother; she's just crazy. I know how to handle her!"

You might respond, "Dad, it sounds like Mom is getting more confused, but I'm glad you've found some things that work for you." This approach allows your father to feel that he is truly being heard.

If you believe your parent has lost their ability to care with kindness, you might have to begin making suggestions. These are best framed in anecdotal statements such as "I have a friend whose wife is just like Mom and what he does to get her in the shower is…" Aging parents are more likely to take advice from their adult children when presented in this non-threatening way.

Anger Can Be a Sign of Other Conditions

If expressing anger is new for your parent, it might signify that they are actually feeling depressed or anxious. It can also be an early sign of dementia. Here, again, active listening can help. You might say, "Mom, you are so angry lately and that is just not like you. Let's see if you have something going on that needs treatment. We can make an appointment with the doctor today." A doctor's visit is important because it's the only way to properly diagnose exactly what is going on.

Don't Get Trapped

Whatever the reason for your parent's anger—or your comfort level in dealing with it—try to avoid impossible-to-win arguments and rationalizations. Wait for a calm moment, and then gently probe for what they are feeling or missing. Ask whether they have any idea what would make them feel better. If they come back with anger, avoid being judgmental. Use active listening to acknowledge their anger and unhappiness and let that be the end of the conversation.

If anger in general has become a major concern, limit your visits and conversations. Be honest about why. You can say, "If you start shouting, I will need to leave or go in the other room." You don't need to tolerate being abused out of some outsized sense of responsibility. You can come back and give the care that is needed, but if an interaction goes south, do what you need to do and move away.

If you become the regular target of a parent's anger, it's time to have a family meeting and divide up tasks. You may need to expand your circle to include friends and outside community resources. No one should have to handle a steady stream of abuse.

Affirmation:

"I am entitled to respect.
I respect others."

CHAPTER EIGHTEEN

Dating and Your Parent

Someone who is in decline still needs affection, intimacy, and other expressions of love. Supporting your parent's desire to seek affection in their later years and begin a new relationship may require adjustments from adult children.

When an aging parent starts dating, their children can often feel uncomfortable. It's important to evaluate why these feelings exist and then take a step back. We all deserve love and yearn for companionship. Romance is natural and healthy, and we need to support life-enhancing relationships.

When your parent finds someone special, they also find a partner—someone to lean on. They have someone to bounce their ideas off of, and with whom they can share their worries and hopes, smiles and tears. Instead of focusing on your own discomfort when Mom or Dad sparks up a late-life romance, try to appreciate that someone is bringing your parent joy.

Once you get past the initial shock that a new person is playing an important role in your parent's life, try to consider the benefits this new companion provides. Their new friend can be there when family isn't available and can relate to them in ways that younger family members may not be able. For example, they can share similar stories and feelings about phases of life, decades past, loss of a spouse, age-related ailments, and more.

There are also health benefits to elderly romance. Having someone to go outside and walk with will inevitably entice your parent to get more fresh air and more exercise. Having someone to talk to and play games with can help keep their mind sharp. A partner can also ease worry or sadness.

When your aging parent finds romance, try to reserve judgment. Keep in mind that your parent may have found a great love, or simply a valuable companion for the last chapter of their life. Think back to when they were skeptical about your boyfriends or girlfriends. You likely wanted your parents to trust you and give your romantic interest a chance. Now it's your turn to make your parent feel like you approve by setting up a time to meet this new partner, get to know them, and help them feel accepted. Social engagement is important for older adults living alone, and if a romance is authentic, it can make the last chapter of Mom or Dad's life very fulfilling.

But the other side of loneliness is gullibility, and "sweetheart scams" use that need for attention as bait to prey upon single or cognitively impaired seniors. They ingratiate themselves into Mom or Dad's life by falsely claiming love and affection, but with the intention to take advantage of their finances, home, or social connections. Perpetrators isolate your parent and indoctrinate them with false stories about their controlling family, until your parent is convinced they only need the new love interest in their life.

If your family member has early to mid-stage dementia, this has to be dealt with quickly to avoid a loss of assets—and the emotional toll it can take on your parent. If you are suspicious of a sweetheart scam, call your local Adult Protective Services agency. Then have bank and investment statements sent to you, as well as to your parent or their accountant, so you can be on the lookout for unusual transactions.

Affirmation:

"I sleep well focusing on the positives."

CHAPTER NINETEEN

Recognizing and Understanding Early Dementia

Early onset dementia frequently causes family discord. Often, one child thinks their parent is just depressed but the other feels this is a significant cognitive change, such as the beginning of Alzheimer's disease. This dilemma is complicated by the fact that only about half of people with mild cognitive impairment develop full dementia.

Knowing the red flags of cognitive decline—and when and where to get an exam or diagnosis—helps you find the trusted resources that can determine the stage of cognitive decline or the type of dementia your parent is showing. Outside resources can also get everyone in the family on the same page in order to move forward in a positive manner.

Identifying Early Dementia

The early signs of progressive dementia often cause tension between family members: differing perceptions come from a complicated mix of history, social conditioning, and each person's current life circumstances.

Siblings often disagree about what is really wrong—some chalk up the mental changes to depression, boredom, a recent illness, or even allergies. These disagreements can delay diagnosis and make a difficult, painful process nearly unbearable.

Early dementia is often mild cognitive impairment (MCI), and only about half of those with this diagnosis move into more progressive dementias. It's understandable if some family members want to dismiss concerns about what's happening to Mom's thinking, communication, or ability to follow a conversation.

If your parent doesn't already have a diagnosis, first explore long-term care insurance. If you apply for long-term care insurance after your parent is diagnosed with dementia, they won't qualify for coverage.

Early diagnosis is important, and you need to move quickly because it allows the person with a progressive illness to be more involved in planning for their future. It's more likely that your family member can take advantage of new medications or clinical trials that might extend the time they can reliably handle daily activities. As the likely primary caregiver, you can better plan for the legal, financial, logistical, and emotional challenges that are sure to follow.

Understanding the Most Prevalent Dementias

Dementia is an impairment that affects memory, information processing, judgment, personality, and language in ways that can deeply impact nearly every aspect of a person's life, including physical safety.

Because the causes of dementia symptoms are varied—reversible illness, like any infection, high blood sugar, or dehydration can cause these symptoms—you must tell either your primary care doctor or a memory screening clinic about all symptoms. Many major or academic medical centers have a memory screening clinic, or you can find one online at the Alzheimer's Association's website or a local teaching university hospital.

Short-term memory loss is usually the first symptom of MCI. While about half the people with this diagnosis progress to one of the four dementias listed below, the other half typically plateau with relatively manageable memory issues.

The four major dementias, however, are progressive and not reversible—at least not yet. Some studies have found that new medications, diet, exercise, social engagement, and mindfulness activities help slow dementia progression.

1. Alzheimer's disease: an irreversible, progressive brain disease that at first slowly destroys memory and thinking skills, and eventually leads to an inability to do the simplest daily tasks. Alzheimer's disease is the most common cause of dementia among older people, and symptoms usually appear after age 65.

2. Lewy Body Dementia: a common form of dementia that can look like both Alzheimer's and Parkinson's diseases, and can be

especially challenging to diagnose correctly. Early symptoms include vivid visual hallucinations, falling, thinking problems, and short-term memory issues as well as periods of clarity.

3. Vascular Dementia: a general term covering brain damage from impaired blood flow or a stroke, although not every stroke causes vascular dementia. Symptoms include problems with reasoning, planning, judgment, memory, and other thought processes.

4. Frontotemporal Dementia (FTD): often is thought to be a mental illness because it starts with people in their fifties and sixties. FTD results from the progressive degeneration of the brain's temporal and frontal lobes—areas responsible for decision-making, behavioral control, emotion, and language. Memory is not impaired in the early stages.

The Value of Early Diagnosis

Once you have a diagnosis, your family can create a realistic care plan for what could be a very long journey. Families that share the care with each other—or paid caregivers—often fare best. Shared arrangements help caregivers find balance in their lives and prevent burnout or stress-related illnesses.

Equally important, early diagnosis can open doors for your family member to be proactive through:

• clinical trials
• healthy diets

- exercise

- mental stimulation

- mindfulness activities (meditation, yoga, nature walks, soft music)

For both patients and their families, it's important to remember that joy happens in the moment. Planning pleasant activities each day helps everyone stay in the moment and find reasons to smile.

Affirmation:

"Life happens with each breath. I bring the gift of life to each day and delight in the littlest of experiences."

CHAPTER TWENTY

Communicating with a Parent with Dementia

Any stage of dementia is a source of enormous stress, for the aging parent and their children. Suddenly having to change lifelong communication habits is often painful for everyone. Knowing how to communicate with a parent in cognitive decline helps protect their self-esteem, reduce anxiety and stress, and avoid many behavioral problems. Substantial resources are available to support you through one of the most challenging aspects of the caregiver journey.

Once a parent has been diagnosed with dementia, you will most likely need to learn new ways to communicate with them. Your goal is to reduce anxiety, protect self-esteem, and convey emotional understanding.

While your parent may find ways to *remember* things—such as writing notes—it will be difficult for them to learn new ways of *doing* things. Be respectful of their methods, but also make sure your parent or their caregiver completes necessary tasks and keeps necessary appointments.

Top Ten Tips for Communicating Effectively

Use the following ten tips to help you with communication challenges:

1. Don't try to reason with a person who has dementia. This can only lead to conflict and/or frustration.

2. Keep information simple. For example, if someone in your family is seriously ill, do not give a lot of details—this will only cause worry. Instead say something like "Mary isn't feeling well, let's send her a card."

3. Do not share future events too far in advance. This can cause anxiety or fear about what to wear, how to get there, or what gift to buy. Give the information a day or two in advance, at most. As the disease progresses, informing your parent on the day of the event is fine and, in some circumstances, only thirty minutes, notice is best.

4. Don't correct misinformation. Self-esteem is at risk in the early and middle stages of this illness. If the misinformation is not putting anyone at risk, just accept it and change the subject.

5. Eliminate multiple choices. Decision making is difficult, so offer only one choice. Instead of saying, "Would you like coffee, tea, or water?" start with the answer most used in the

past: "Would you like a cup of coffee?" The same goes with food, clothing, and outings.

6. Give only one direction at a time. For example, "Can you bring me the paper?" or "Can you put the plates on the table?" rather than "Can you take the paper off the table and then set the table with the dishes and silverware?"

7. Simplify your language. Instead of relying on pronouns, refer to people by their given names. Write down the language and nouns regularly used by your parent and pass this information on to any care providers. For example, do they refer to the bathroom as "the toilet," "the can," or "the head"?

8. Play along. If your parent suffers with delusions, go with it as long as it doesn't jeopardize anyone's safety. For example, if they talk about someone returning who died long ago, you can simply say it will be nice to see him or her again. Or, you can share a memory about that person and then change the subject.

9. Use therapeutic fiblets (little lies) to reduce stress. While it may feel wrong to stretch the truth, sometimes it's the only successful strategy to manage anxiety, protect self-esteem, and deal with resistance to change. For example, when someone with dementia is living alone, but is at significant risk and refuses to relocate, you can use a fiblet like "The neighborhood is having a serious plumbing problem and we need to find you a place for the short term." Avoid committing to a time frame. If your parent asks when they can go home, say that the plumbing issue still has not been fixed. In the meantime, create distractions and new routines for their new

setting. Or maybe you need to get your parent to a doctor's appointment, but they refuse to go. You might tell them that you are going to run errands to the dry cleaners, the florist, and one other stop.

10. As dementia progresses, it is very important to get right in front of the person so they can see you as you speak. It is usually comforting to lightly touch their hand as you talk to them. Because the ability to understand language diminishes as the disease progresses, touch and eye contact can be important forms of communication.

Be creative and pay close attention to body language. If a parent tells you that they feel fine but has their head down and tears in their eyes, take their hand or give them a hug. Say something like "It looks like you are sad." Listen to them, offer a comforting touch, and then, perhaps, suggest a simple activity they can do, such as putting flowers in a vase.

Affirmation:

"I communicate with sensitivity and respect to my family member struggling with their memory loss."

Part Four

Housing
and Travel

CHAPTER TWENTY-ONE

Understanding Available Housing Options

Many older adults may be able to stay at home for all or most of their lives if financial resources and skilled care are available. If not, various levels of assisted living exist, up to and including skilled nursing facilities for the most impaired elders.

Your parent's diagnosis, prognosis, financial resources, and personal preference all determine which assisted living choice is best. This very difficult decision will be easier if you use available resources.

Understandably, many older adults prefer to age in their own home. While this sounds ideal, it is not always in their best interest. Consider the following reasons you should consider alternative living arrangements:

- In-home care is expensive. Many families find that after exploring all local programs and entitlements, they simply do not have the financial resources.

- Staying at home can be socially isolating. This could significantly harm your parent's mental and physical health. Moving to a retirement community would supply safety, activity, and regular human contact.

- Dementia can jeopardize health and safety. Alzheimer's disease and related disorders can make daily decisions impossible for your family member. Fortunately, the availability of housing designed specifically for those with dementia is on the rise.

- The neighborhood may have become more dangerous. Even if you can afford in-home care, caregivers might refuse to take assignments in such neighborhoods.

- Family lives too far away to visit regularly. A move closer to adult children and grandchildren could offer a better quality of life.

- Houses are too big. Many older adults find their long-time homes challenging to maintain and want to downsize. Retirement living may offer a lifestyle that better suits their current desires and abilities.

Exploring Your Options

First, discover the local support systems where your parent lives—there may be many available. Find them through your local Area Agency on Aging or Eldercare Locator. Another option is to see if your area has a Village—a nonprofit network of older adults who help each other through friendship, volunteer assistance, expert guidance, and recommended services.

If you believe staying at home is the best option for Mom or Dad, refer to "Chapter 22: Making Home Care Work." If you are not sure, consult a professional geriatric care manager (PGCM) to be sure your decision will serve your parent's needs as they age.

If a move from the home is the best choice, you have an expanding array of available options, which include retirement communities, independent senior housing, skill nursing facilities, etc.

Retirement communities offer independent living with social and physical activities such as tennis, golf, and swimming. In most cases, your parent would own their condo or apartment, but some communities offer month-to-month rentals. Similarly, independent senior housing complexes are not licensed to provide care, but they can range from low-income federal housing (where seniors pay 25% of their monthly income for rent) to luxurious complexes with many amenities. They often have shared dining and social activities.

Life Care Centers of America or continuing care retirement communities offer tiered levels of guaranteed care at a price. Residents pay a large entry fee—usually ranging from $100,000 up to $1,000,000—as well as monthly fees. Seniors are promised life care ranging from independent living to assisted and skilled nursing care.

Assisted living communities typically offer monthly rentals and many levels of care—or no care—depending on the needs of the individual. They are generally fee-for-service arrangements. Since they do provide care and often manage medications, most states license these facilities but do not require them to have a nurse on staff. When choosing assisted living, ask lots of questions and have an outside party read any agreement before you sign it.

Dementia-specific arrangements are often found on one floor of an assisted living facility—if not in a separate building. These facilities have programs and staff trained to work with those with severe memory loss. Most have "wander-protection"—residents wear bracelets that set off alarms if they cross into a protected area. Dementia-specific arrangements usually cost more than assisted living, and most residents live in shared units.

Small family homes are also called board and care homes. In most states, they are licensed much like assisted living, and typically house about six individuals. Most board and care homes have some private rooms. These homes can be a good choice for those who can't manage long hallways or walks to the dining room. They may need more one-on-one care, or don't enjoy the large social functions that are often a part of assisted living arrangements.

Skilled nursing facilities, sometimes referred to as rehabilitation centers, provide for people whose medical needs exceed the capacity of assisted living facilities. Though skilled nursing facilities were once associated with long-term care, that is less common now. Assisted living facilities have beefed up their ability to care for individuals, even those on hospice care.

Hospice provides 24/7 care at the end of life. It is delivered in a variety of settings, but hospice organizations have begun creating hospice-specific facilities. Hospice licensing laws differ from state to state, so know what services can legally be offered in whichever setting you choose. Most hospice services are covered by Medicare and other insurance, and some services are non profit and some are for-profit.

How to Choose the Right Housing Option

Sorting through these options is not always easy. Often, the first thing is to look at your financial picture and see which of the options are affordable.

Next, project possible future needs. Someone with a degenerative disease like Parkinson's might be doing fine now, but you should consider a care option that can provide more assistance as the disease progresses.

It's critical to base any decision on your parent's values, even if they have advanced dementia. Choose an option that offers some of the pleasures or ambiance you know Mom or Dad enjoys (or enjoyed when they were well).

If you are choosing a licensed facility, check with the local oversight agency, usually an ombudsmen's office. Many are located at, or contract with, your local Area Agency on Aging.

Hospital discharge planners, geriatric care managers, or perhaps your parent's physician can give you recommendations and resources. Support groups can help—others who have made these care decisions could give you new options or information.

Finally, there are so-called "free" agencies that assist with placement. These agencies are mostly staffed with salespeople—not medical or aging experts. You don't pay them, but they receive large commissions from the communities they represent.

Moving a parent to a care facility is an emotional decision. Make the transition easier—and ultimately more successful—by doing your homework. And remember: there are very few things that can't be undone.

Affirmation:

~~~~~~~~~~

"I am imperfect, but I have researched my options and will recalibrate if needed."

CHAPTER TWENTY-TWO

Making Home Care Work

Bringing an outside caregiver into a parent's home carries with it a difficult paradox. On the one hand, parents often fight having an outsider in their home. On the other hand, it may be their only option for remaining in their own home, relatively independent and safe.

Encouraging your parent to accept help, introducing that help, and engaging your parent in making this new relationship work is a delicate dance. Use the various resources in your area to find good care, supervise that care to support its success, and know who to consult with regarding pay, taxes, and worker's compensation.

M ost of us cherish our privacy, and over 80 percent of Americans want to stay in their own homes all their lives. But for your aging family member to do so, you might need to bring in-home care. Maybe a hospital discharge coordinator or physician has said it's time to bring in help. Or maybe you see your frail parent is now at risk for dementia or a progressive illness like Parkinson's or multiple sclerosis.

An older family member with declining abilities might not be able to see the need for in-home care and will resist anyone except family. Try to imagine being in their situation and how challenging it would be to have a stranger in your personal space.

To make home care work for those who don't have dementia, provide rational reasons why this in-home help will allow them to have "life their way" at home. In most cases, you can introduce help slowly—start with a few hours, a few times a week. This often makes accepting help much easier than starting with full eight-hour or twelve-hour shifts, or twenty-four-hour care.

For family members with mild cognitive impairment, you might need to find other titles for caregiver because it implies that your parent is no longer capable. Create a strategy for success by having a written plan that clearly defines all caregiving expectations for your parent's needs and safety.

Many elders accept help more easily if you say you're going to find them a personal assistant to accompany them on errands and assist with some organization. Or refer to the caregiver as a cook, driver, housekeeper, personal trainer, organizer, or pet walker. This gently introduces a caregiver who will likely do much more than these titles imply.

Many families begin by slowly working up to paying a caregiver for 20 hours a week. Day one might simply be a short introduction to the new "cook" or "pet walker." About two days after that first short meeting, the caregiver could come again for tea and cookies. Maybe you can leave to do an errand, allowing time for the two of them to chat for an hour or more. On the third visit, the caregiver might just drop by for a while with a food item to share. Tell the caregiver what your family member's favorite meal is so they can come by on the fourth visit with all the ingredients to make it.

If you can achieve that comfort level, you are probably at the point where the helper can easily work those 20 hours. Of course, there is no generic recipe—you will have to figure out your own approach, but the point is to build the relationship as creatively as you can.

But older family members often find ways to discontinue these services, forcing families to try a number of different agencies. Sometimes the termination happens because a home-care agency doesn't have field supervision or professional care managers (such as nurses, social workers, and gerontologists). If you have not had caregiver success, start by looking for an agency that provides these professional services. It may add to your up-front costs but could also increase your chances of success.

You have a few ways to hire or schedule home care:

- Choose to use family members (either volunteer or hired). Create a schedule with adequate time off to prevent burnout.

- Hire someone privately. Private hires come with some liability to you, so get expert advice. You must be aware of and follow relevant labor laws, or risk hefty fines.

- Let an agency find caregivers for you. A licensed or state-regulated agency pays all taxes, insurances, and benefits required. They also provide supervision and training for their caregivers. And in the event of your caregiver calling in sick, the agency can find a replacement. There are registries of caregivers but they don't pay taxes and insurances—ask questions and reduce your liability by knowing who is liable for any breaches in the law or if an accident should occur.

All of these can be challenging choices. Be sure to do your homework and don't be afraid to ask questions before choosing any type of care. If you have been unsuccessful, find a professional partner or support group to assist you through the process.

Above all, your goal is to provide safety, peace, and quality of life to your parent who needs the care.

Affirmation:

"I rest in knowing my care will be extended with the right team players."

CHAPTER TWENTY-THREE

Driving Safety and Your Parent

At some point, your parent will probably not be able to drive safely. This effect on elder independence is another difficult juncture. Caregivers must assess safety concerns, evaluate other transportation options, and often reconcile differing opinions about this issue among family members.

Taking the keys away from an aging parent is a difficult passage from independence to increasing dependence. After all, having our own transportation and the ability to run errands at any time is personal freedom. Taking away your parent's ability to drive can feel like you're taking away their dignity.

Everyone ages at a different pace, with different disabilities and ailments. There is no set age at which a senior should be banned from driving—it's possible to drive a vehicle well into the golden years. What matters most is medical fitness.

While medication and chronic conditions that limit mobility—such as arthritis—could impair your parent's driving ability, some driving skills just become more difficult for senior drivers. Making left turns, driving in the dark, merging into traffic, changing lanes, yielding to traffic, or following traffic signals are often problematic because of other risk factors like visual decline, hearing loss, or declining motor skills.

Dementia affects all brain functions, and physicians in many states must report a diagnosis to the local Department of Motor Vehicles (DMV). Some states even have systems for anonymously reporting unsafe drivers, which then require the driver to go in for testing.

Regular medical checkups—including vision and hearing tests—help ensure that older adults are still capable of driving safely. If you're concerned about significant changes, talk to your doctor. A family physician will often order an evaluation or make a referral to a driving clinic where an occupational therapist will assess your parent's ability to drive.

If you fear Mom or Dad should turn in their driver's license, carefully consider how to approach the conversation. Emphasize that for their safety—and that of others on the road—it may be time for them to change their habits and consider other transportation options. A first change could be their agreement to avoid freeways or to refrain from driving at night.

Their decision-making capability could also be an issue in this conversation, and a consultation with an elder law attorney or legal services for seniors could help. To avoid a parent's anger toward you or your siblings, bring in a geriatric care manager or family therapist to introduce the upcoming changes. These professionals can also help adult children understand and respect different approaches to the problem.

Resources such as Uber, Lyft, and GoGoGrandparent are on the rise in the over-65 generation. And remember, many communities have senior transportation services.

Affirmation:

"I did not take the car away
from Dad. His disease took away
his ability to drive."

CHAPTER TWENTY-FOUR

Deciding to Move from Home

Sometimes it is no longer safe or reasonable for an aging parent to live at home. Other times, caregiving needs exceed available resources and selling the home is the only viable long-term option. Families need to discuss the possibility of moving, and work with their parent to come to grips with what is often a wrenching change in their life.

Just thinking about moving an elder out of their home can be incredibly difficult and fraught with emotion for both the elder and their adult children. But when you have safety concerns, or it's clear that your parent's home environment is not supporting healthy independence, it is time to think about moving a parent to a more supportive environment in their community—or closer to a family member.

The following red flags indicate it may be time to move:

- You have exhausted available community resources
- You have tried home care but your parent always finds a way to let the help go
- Your parent's safety is at risk
- The family caregiver is overly caring for your parent, working around the clock or rejecting help from others
- Two parents have dementia, and neither can truly care for the other
- Your parent's home or neighborhood is not conducive to handicapped living—too many stairs, a changing community, or limited access to transportation or shopping
- Your parent does not have a local advocate/family member
- Your parent is frequently hospitalized

Family members with progressive illnesses might need to move sooner rather than later. Earlier moves give elders and their family a longer time to enjoy life before health deteriorates and their care needs escalate to skilled nursing. But someone with mild dementia (or other illnesses) often acclimates and can stay at the assisted-living care level longer than someone with a more progressed illness.

Before you consider moving Mom or Dad from their home, first look at the existing financial resources. You want to know from the start what your parent can afford and how long they can afford it.

Explore your parent's local choices, as well as those close to you. If finances are tight, you might find more care options at a lower monthly rent in more rural areas. But you will need to visit these communities, so consider the time and resources that commute might take.

In senior living, each state differs slightly in what they call the various levels of licensed care. Most states offer assisted living communities, small residential care homes (private homes in neighborhoods), freestanding Alzheimer's care homes, and skilled nursing homes. Less frail, more active seniors might manage well in non-licensed senior housing facilities.

Some areas also have continuing care retirement communities (CCRC). They often have a buy-in and provide all levels of care, and most people enter while they are fully functioning. CCRCs are an ideal choice for elders who do not have adult children and like receiving all of their care in one complex. Depending on the CCRC, you can still consider this kind of facility even if your parent is no longer completely independent. Times are changing—many facilities take residents in their skilled nursing centers on a monthly fee basis.

Across the country, the federal government's Housing and Urban Development (HUD) offers senior housing for low- to middle-income seniors. However, these facilities do not provide any nursing or medical care. In many cases, housing consists of a one-bedroom apartment, and may have a built-in emergency response system. In some HUD housing communities for those over sixty years old, Mom or Dad can opt-in to activities or a dining program for an additional cost.

An elder's local support systems could be a significant reason to keep them in their own community. Moving them away from their neighborhood to be closer to a family member might result in a heavy burden for care coordination—many families struggle to balance the demands of their own nuclear family and/or career with these new caregiving duties.

When your older parent is not interested in moving, starting the conversation requires a delicate approach. Using a geriatric care manager can be a tremendous help.

Affirmation:

"I find answers to challenging questions from experts in the field. I base my choices on their resources and the longstanding values of my older family member."

CHAPTER TWENTY-FIVE

Choosing a New Place to Live

Complex and overlapping considerations can make selecting a new home for an aging parent difficult. It's important to determine the types of support your parent will need, the facility's location, transportation options, social and religious offerings, and financial compatibility. To make the best decision, you will need to ask questions—of yourself and the retirement facilities you consider.

O nce your family decides it's time to move Mom or Dad from their home into a more supportive environment, your family needs to make a number of decisions. Just be sure you have legal authority before deciding anything for an older family member who is cognitively compromised.

They will need help choosing a facility, organizing the move, and adjusting to their new home. If they move a distance away, you'll also need to find new medical providers and identify where your family member will do everyday activities—shopping, socializing, and volunteering.

Before choosing a retirement setting, answer the following questions:

1. Does your parent need support now? What kind of support does he or she need (i.e., bathing, medication, diet, dressing, pet care)?

2. If your parent is independent and doesn't need support now, do they have any diagnosis that could progress and require support later?

3. Does your parent still drive? If so, what are the parking arrangements?

4. Does your parent have a special diet? Can the community provide that?

5. Will the facility allow a small pet?

6. Will your parent need transportation to appointments? How will the facility accommodate these?

7. If your parent is hospitalized, do you still have to pay for levels of care, even when Mom or Dad is outside the community?

8. What emergency plans are in place?

9. What nighttime staff is on duty?

10. Is there a nurse on staff? If not, how are medications managed and by whom—is this person trained?

11. How does the facility welcome new residents?

12. What in-house activities are available? Are the activities ones your parent will enjoy? Will the facility transport residents to events in the community?

13. Are there religious services on site, or do they take people to places of worship in the community?

14. Ask about the ratio of men to women. It's not always a plus to be the only guy in the place!

15. Ask about the process they used during the coronavirus pandemic for keeping residents safe at the same time as keeping them stimulated and connected to friends and/or family.

16. Ask any other questions specific to your family member.

You should have a list of pros and cons for each community. Use this list to narrow down your choices and be sure to visit more than once—and at least once without an appointment. Before you make a final choice, check with the local ombudsman about any citations and serious issues regarding the community. You can find them through your state's Office of Aging.

Affirmation:

"I am comfortable and at ease. I look
forward to positives every day."

CHAPTER TWENTY-SIX

Helping Your Parent Cope with Moving

Think about your first apartment or new home, and you will probably recall how stressful moving is, even when it's something you want. For older adults, moving is even more stressful—especially when they are resistant or when care issues and/or cognitive needs force them to relocate. Your parent may express their stress through anger, depression, or various types of acting out, and you'll need to factor that emotional toll into the move logistics.

Reduce the stress by considering all the potential logistical challenges and using professional resources.

The more time you put into planning the move, the less stress for everyone involved. If you have done your homework and chosen a community for your family member, you should have some ideas of floor plan, necessary items to bring, and what not to include. Remember that—in terms of square footage and compared to your parent's former home—retirement community apartments are usually small.

If you use a professional move manager, they can help with tactics for de-cluttering beforehand and sorting what will go with Mom or Dad to the new facility. If you need help and are feeling overwhelmed, contact the National Association of Senior Move Managers.

If you do the planning yourself, focus on what is necessary to get your family member settled into the new location—you can think about what to store, sell, or give away later on. Trying to do everything at the same time will just add stress to the move, and in some cases, your elder might become overwhelmed by too many decisions and refuse to move.

For family members with dementia, it's important that the new living space is set up as closely as possible to how it was in their home. But even when the new setup resembles the former one, your parent may still wonder how their things got moved. Make your response simple and use distraction—talk about something else in the room or take a walk and then come back to the new room. In many facilities, you can hire a personal caregiver to help someone get settled—to arrange and rearrange items until your parent is comfortable in the new setting.

If you hire a caregiver, be sure they take your family member to community meals and events. At these events, the caregiver should tell your parent they will be right back, then watch them from a distance. This prevents your parent from building a dependence on the caregiver and helps Mom or Dad form relationships with the other residents, so the new community becomes a place of companionship and joy.

It is common for older adults to be unhappy with this type of move at first because everything is unfamiliar, and they can feel lonely. If Mom or Dad tells you they don't like the new setting, you don't need to act right away. Nor should you try to tell them about all the beautiful things or events they can go to. Instead, use active listening. Say something like "I hear it's hard for you to be in your new setting," then reassure them you can discuss this in more detail the next time you visit.

At the same time, try to engage the help of the senior community. They run into this reaction often and can work with other residents to help ease your parent's transition. One common technique is to ask a new resident for help with something, so they feel a sense of purpose.

If your parent is angry or feels betrayed because they wanted to stay in their home but could not because of financial or safety concerns, you may feel guilty. Don't let guilt pull you into visiting every day—it creates a dependence on you and hampers your parent's ability to make new friends. If you need help accepting that the move was truly necessary, find a support group.

If after three to four months your family member is still feeling depressed or grieving the loss of their former home, consider bringing in a professional counselor. Most senior communities have a list of local licensed counselors who work with seniors and will come to the home. Or talk to your parent's doctor about a short-term prescription for an antidepressant. For a competent senior, relocation could be especially hard—it's common for them to need both counseling and medication to adjust and find interests that bring them joy and satisfaction. Seniors with mild dementia could also benefit from counseling, but those with advanced dementia might need a more detailed, medically approved plan of care to adjust.

Sometimes, the senior community can offer referrals to professionals or organizations that can help with the move, as well as those that can help with the adjustment.

Affirmation:

"My love and care guide my choices,
and I let go of guilt."

Part Five

Family
Dynamics

CHAPTER TWENTY-SEVEN

Family Traditions and Expectations

Each family has its own traditions and values—often drawn from specific cultural expectations—which guide their care for an aging parent. In today's rapidly changing world, the demands of caring for a parent often challenge strongly held cultural or familial traditions and generate enormous anger or sadness.

Distance, jobs, or other obligations can conflict with these traditions. Working with a counselor who knows the family's culture helps each person understand how broken rules can transform into new and healthy ways for the family to support each other.

Most families have unwritten rules and cultural traditions that prescribe how to care for an aging parent, but these can conflict with modern caregiving—as well as with your parent's expectations.

Until we face a dilemma that creates an emotional crisis, we are often not aware that these rules affect how we think about caregiving. The guilt of having to place Mom or Dad in a care facility—especially if you come from a tradition that has always demanded caring for elders in your home—can send many family members to counseling.

Respecting Cultural and Religious Traditions

Some cultural or religious traditions frown on discussing end-of-life concerns, much less the idea of death. This complicates the younger generation's ability to make decisions that sync with their aging parents' intimate wishes and beliefs.

Many religious traditions are also quite specific about what to do from the beginning of an illness through the time after death. If your parent has strong religious or cultural beliefs, it's important to learn—as early as possible—what those beliefs systems say about death and dying. To ease the stress of this conversation, read about the traditions or talk with a religious leader in your community.

Respecting Family Traditions

Family rules and relationships can get especially complicated as they come into play during the caregiving journey. Sibling rivalries and patterns that took root years before can suddenly rear their ugly heads.

Look for Early Warning Signs

To effectively navigate cultural traditions that are complicating your caregiving journey, try to recognize the following early clues:

1. Do you find yourself grumbling about your parent's religious values or cultural traditions?

2. Are extended family members pressing you to respect cultural traditions in the care of your parent?

3. Are you feeling guilty because you can't make your older family member happy?

4. Are you angry with another family member for not doing what you expected them to do for your elder?

5. Do you get a "stomachache" every time your sibling or a particular relative calls you?

6. Do you feel anger, frustration, guilt, sadness, and/or depression if you can't follow family tradition and care for the elder in your home?

7. You want to be an advocate for your family member, but they will not give you legal access and no one else has been named.

8. Your parent has told you their desires, but they conflict with previous generations' decisions.

If you are the decision maker, solicit as much guidance and input as you can from your family, Mom or Dad's community, and your own. Then make the best decision you can at the time. Licensed counselors, professional geriatric care managers, religious leaders, medical experts, and support groups are the best resources for these hard decisions, but in most cases there are no easy answers.

Hopefully, your willingness to listen carefully will free you from the crippling guilt that often plagues the ones who must make the hard decisions. Professional counseling can help you understand that you acted with the best intentions and as much information as possible.

Affirmation:

"My love is endless; my energy is limited."

CHAPTER TWENTY-EIGHT

Working Through Differences

Even in the most well-meaning situations, adult children can seriously disagree over what is best for their parent. Adult children can have different points of view about everything—from preserving the estate, to keeping the family home, or moving a parent to supportive living. Families get stuck, the parent becomes anxious, and things can quickly turn bitter. Far too often, these disagreements end a lifetime of positive and meaningful relations.

Using valuable resources can save family relationships by showing adult children how to agree to disagree and get their parents' needs met without destroying the family system.

Siblings often disagree on the care needs of their aging parents. One may feel their parent needs no care at all, while another feels Mom or Dad needs ten times the amount of care to stay safe and well. This conflict can delay an intervention that would benefit everyone.

It can be hard to accept that a parent's abilities are declining enough that they need intervention. It is also hard to insist that a parent needs help—especially if they are resistant to receiving care because it might lead to moving them from their beloved home. Consulting a professional geriatric care manager or attending a class for family caregivers can help multiple family members hear the same information and make more informed decisions.

If the family already works well together around compromising on major decisions, an honest conversation should bring about a solution or a process everyone can agree upon. Give yourselves a window of time to accomplish a specific goal—and a plan B if the first idea doesn't pan out. Schedule a follow-up within two months of the first family meeting to discuss what worked and what didn't, as well as next steps.

However, if your family and/or parent have always had a hard time making decisions, find a professional mediator or a skilled family therapist who can guide the conversation and ensure everyone is heard and respected. All parties going into the meeting need to be open to compromise and to following meeting rules.

To help focus on the issues and not get tied up in the ghosts of past family dysfunction, each adult child should answer two important questions before the meeting:

1. Who and what are you most concerned about?

2. What do you want to be the outcome of today's session?

With these answers you can prioritize and work toward a solution for each issue as a group. If someone doesn't follow the rules of the meeting, they should be asked to leave so the others can find a compromise that helps Mom or Dad.

To confirm that everyone is on the same page, ensure that they can say in their own words what decision was made, and who will take the necessary actions. Doing this at the end of each meeting keeps the meeting focused on your parents and is respectful.

Affirmation:

"I reduce stress by having plans that support peaceful family interactions."

CHAPTER TWENTY-NINE

Confronting Greed

Most people want what is best for their parent—sadly, some
try to use their parents' assets for their own retirement or
current lifestyle. Confronting the self-serving adult child and
dealing with the legal issues that come from that can make
these situations difficult and painful.

C aring for an aging family member is emotionally challenging.
But it can take a financial toll as well, especially when family
members realize that the person overseeing parental finances has a
lot of control and may not be using it well. How they spend or do
not spend money can be an ugly issue to confront because adult
children often have differing opinions on what is financially best.

On the one hand, the person in control of that money is legally
liable. Overspending can lead to charges of elder abuse, which is
punishable by prison and fines. But some siblings may think funds

are plentiful. Or they may not understand that with quality support, Mom or Dad could live longer—and their care cost more—than expected. Financial restraint is required to ensure the funds and assets your parent accumulated over a lifetime are used for their life and care, according to their values and needs.

On the other hand, there is a fine balance between being prudent and ensuring that a parent receives what they need. Not spending money for your parent's health and welfare could be considered neglect, especially if other siblings or the authorities feel it's motivated by a desire to preserve that money for an inheritance.

If you suspect someone is mishandling funds and not providing proper care—and you are a co-beneficiary of the estate—you can ask for an accounting of your parents' assets. If the person resists, you might call your local Adult Protective Services agency (APS), a division of most county social services departments.

When your family can't come to an agreement on a care plan, you may need to rely on professional help. Find a mediator who specializes in these types of conflicts or can suggest a third-party private fiduciary, such as a court-ordered guardianship or conservatorship. Or seek out an attorney who can take self-serving adult children or other individuals to court.

To preserve your family relationships, gently confront concerns and try to avoid getting personal. Focus on the elder and their needs. If necessary, bring in the experts, who may lower both the emotional and financial costs in the long run.

Affirmation:

"I ask questions of others and receive
respect. I secure advice from professionals."

Part Six

The Emotional Health of Caregivers

Dealing with Caregiver Guilt

Unhealthy guilt is one of the biggest traps for adult children of aging parents. Its power to stimulate overly caring makes it a powerful brake on a family's ability to move forward through the caregiving journey. Fortunately, there are methods that help overcome the guilt adult children can experience.

When you're forced to intervene for someone who has been capable and in control their whole lives, it often causes feelings of guilt or even shame. For adult children in the role of family caregiver, such feelings are common.

Guilt can result from either intentionally doing something hurtful, or from simply forgetting or ignoring something harmful. This type of healthy guilt usually requires a form of forgiveness and/or repayment. In its most positive light, it creates learning opportunities. Making amends can allow us to move on with our lives.

Family members who turn over a parent's daily care—or place them in a care setting—experience a type of unhealthy guilt. To remove it, you must remember why you had to make this change, then allow yourself to experience those feelings that underlie the guilt—including sadness, grief, and even anger.

The third type of guilt results in what some refer to as over-caring. This type of unhealthy guilt often arises out of a need to repay a parent or family member for the care they gave you. Or it can arise because you're trying to inspire the love your parent never expressed when you were younger, and now may never be able to give you. In turn, your health and other relationships could suffer. If you tell family and friends that Mom or Dad will only let you care for them—and give 101 reasons why you can't hire care or find an assisted living option—you could be what I refer to as "over-caring."

Guilt that compels over-caring may require professional help or a support group to help you understand why you hold on to this role and don't share—or release—the caregiving demands. Remember, you did not inflict the dementia, stroke, or other cause of your parent's current condition—and despite your best efforts, they need more care than you can provide. If you find that your guilt interferes with sleep, work, or quality of life, seek professional counseling.

Spending time doing things you enjoy can ease the guilt and help you be at your best, so you can continue to advocate for and provide loving support to your parent. If you find yourself stuck in unhealthy guilt, practice self-care—join a support group, take walks, swim, have lunch with friends, or do something you enjoy. Mindfulness practices like meditation or yoga may be helpful as well.

Affirmation:

"I rest assured that I will live every day of
my life with meaning and value."

CHAPTER THIRTY-ONE

Identifying Caregiver Depression

Witnessing a parent's difficult slide toward the end of life
often causes sadness and depression for adult children.
Many people experience more grief before their parent
passes than after. Sadness is a normal reaction, but before
it slides into clinical depression—especially common due
to caregiver stress—find help. Celebrating your parent
while they are still living can ease both stress and sadness.

Caring for a family member is a challenge on many levels—
physical, financial, emotional, or all three—and these stressors
can put caregivers through an emotional roller coaster.

Depression is an understandable emotional reaction to the grief
we feel when we experience or anticipate a loss. When you are caring

for Mom or Dad, you are actually grieving their loss of self-sufficiency, as well as the loss of what your relationship once was (or even what you'd wished it to be).

Caregivers tend to focus on what their parent needs, not what they are missing personally—from a hug, to advice, to shared memories. The caregiving burden often leads to fatigue, a sense of sadness, and a longing for what the fading relationship used to be.

When a caregiver does not acknowledge and address these feelings, they easily move into depression. Many people think depression is nonstop sadness, crying, and retreating to bed. But a family caregiver doesn't have that luxury. Instead, we often see a behavior known as agitated depression. The caregiver becomes overly active, filling every moment with tasks in order to ignore or skirt their real feelings. Too often, this type of depression leads to the caregiver forgetting medical appointments, social events, and exercise—all important aspects of a healthy mental and physical state.

Research tells us that at least 50 percent of those caring for someone with dementia wind up being diagnosed with clinical depression. Too often, it goes untreated, leading to eating disorders, weight gain or loss, sleep difficulty, high blood pressure or more serious heart conditions, cancer, and other stress-related disorders.

To diagnose clinical depression, many doctors use the symptoms for major depressive disorders listed in the American Psychiatric Association's Diagnostic and Statistical Manual of Mental Disorders (DSM-5).

Signs and symptoms of clinical depression may include the following:

- Persistent sadness, tearfulness, emptiness, or hopelessness

- Angry outbursts, irritability, or frustration, even over small matters

- Lost interest or pleasure in most or all normal activities, such as sex, hobbies, or sports

- Sleep disturbances including insomnia or sleeping too much

- Tiredness and lack of energy, so even small tasks take extra effort

- Reduced appetite and weight loss, or increased cravings for food and weight gain

- Anxiety, agitation, or restlessness

- Slowed thinking, concentration, difficulty making decisions or remembering things

- Frequent or recurrent thoughts of death, suicidal thoughts or attempts

- Unexplained physical problems, such as backaches or headaches

Symptoms are usually severe enough to cause noticeable problems in relationships with others, or in day-to-day activities such as work, school, or social activities.

Remember, depression can run in families, hit you hard, and send you into an emotional tailspin. This affects your parent's care, which is why it's so important that you take care of yourself.

On airplanes, flight attendants say to put the oxygen mask on yourself first before helping someone dependent on you. Keep this in mind when you are focusing on self-care. You cannot give good care if you are depressed or overwhelmed. Seek treatment—or at least be sure to have some joy in your life.

There are a number of things like the following that you can do to help alleviate caregiver depression:

1. Own the problem—label your feelings correctly

2. Seek help—ask your physician for a referral to a therapist who understands caregiving stress

3. Ask for an antidepressant, even if just short term

4. Attend a support group for family caregivers

5. Keep a journal—writing often becomes cathartic, allowing you to release your feelings into the written word

6. Be sure every day has one activity just for you (examples could include walking the dog, taking a bubble bath, allowing time to read a few chapters of a good novel, taking a yoga class, or learning mindfulness activities)

7. Be specific when you ask for help from other family members: "Can you take Dad to his dentist appointments?" Or "I would like your help arranging for a landscaper to take a tree down."

8. Be sure you have a long-term plan for your family member *and* yourself, or you may end up with underlying stress you don't recognize (if not addressed, it can move into depression)

9. That early morning or evening walk is good for your health, spirit, and mind

10. Diet is often a big factor in depression, and sugar and carbohydrates will add to the problem, so eat a good, heart-healthy diet with lots of fresh foods

11. Meditation and mindfulness activities can also help, so pick one of our affirmations and repeat it to yourself throughout the day and try listening to a meditation before going to sleep

It's not a sin to be less than perfect or less than a superhero. Grief is normal—you will feel sadness, but depression is different and can be treated. It helps no one if you get too sick to do right by your parent. Finding a balance between self-care and caregiving will help everyone in the circle of care.

Affirmation:

"I have made changes that enhance my well-being and happiness."

CHAPTER THIRTY-TWO

Experiencing Caregiver Anger

As the difficult demands of caregiving set in, frustration, sadness, and guilt can quickly morph into anger and *resentment*. While anger is a normal, well-documented step in the grief process, it is also the least understood of depression's underlying emotions. Free yourself from anger so you can move forward with the caregiving journey.

The majority of caregivers would not be telling the truth if they said they never experienced anger when caregiving. Instead, many will say they're "frustrated" or even "disappointed." But anger is a much deeper—and valid—emotion. What we do with it is key for being a mentally healthy, mature adult.

Here are five critical steps for dealing with anger:

1. Acknowledge your anger to at least one other person. For instance: your parent refuses your advice and then suffers a consequence, something that might mean more work or worry for you. Share that feeling with a friend or other family member. You are not being unfair to Mom or Dad, you're being honest about yourself.

2. Ask yourself if the anger regarding the incident at hand is valid. If not, consider what else is going on in your life. Is it possible the anger is being caused by a parent asking the same question ten times and then you finally shout at her? If you shout at her, is it really because of the situation, or because you're angry that you're not getting support from other family members?

3. If possible, step away, take a walk, or go into another room before returning to respond to a situation.

4. Try to determine who or what you are angry at. In the example above, are you releasing stress by shouting at Mom instead of being angry with your sibling who—when you ask for help—just says how busy they are traveling? Learn to take a deep breath and re-phrase your request that they step up and do something to help you balance your caregiving duties.

5. Before you work on this problem, try to forgive the people involved. Forgiveness is key to not letting anger progress into guilt or depression. Sometimes, it is self-forgiveness that will release you.

Caregivers are often saints who just get overwhelmed at times, and anger is a valid emotion that can come from feeling burnt out. When you express anger inappropriately, forgive yourself. Keep a journal or talk to someone who can give you permission to be human, with emotions that need attention.

Affirmation:

"Every day I take the opportunity
to re-create and improve myself."

CHAPTER THIRTY-THREE

Tips for Caregivers Who Experienced Abuse in the Past

Victims of abuse should approach caregiving with eyes wide open and with professional guidance, because abuse is often hidden or unacknowledged. Protect yourself and your aging parent by honestly facing your feelings of anger or resentment and find resources to help you prevent becoming an abuser.

It is hard to sacrifice time, energy, and dollars to someone who harmed you or wasn't there for you in the past. Resentment, anger, disdain, and even guilt will color your ability to provide care. Sometimes adult children tend to overly care in an attempt to gain the love they missed in their youth.

But to provide good, ethical care to a parent who abused or neglected you, you need to sort through these complex feelings.

Try the following suggestions for the best possible outcome for you and your parent:

- Find a local support group for adult children of aging parents
- Seek professional counseling
- Recognize and acknowledge your own needs
- If you cannot give the care yourself because of emotions or other restrictions, find outside agencies to oversee your parent's care

Affirmation:

"My well-being is a priority, and I team with experts for the best outcomes."

CHAPTER THIRTY-FOUR

"The Only One" Syndrome

"The only one" syndrome is common in adult children who care for their aging parents. Telling signs are comments such as "My mother won't let anyone else do her shopping," or "If I don't visit Dad in the nursing home, he won't eat." These caregivers often resist sharing the load with anyone and believe they are the only ones who care enough to do what needs to be done. But they often wind up doing more harm than good when they trap themselves in that position.

One of the biggest hurdles in caring for another person—especially a frail older parent—is overcoming the sense that you are the only one who can provide care the right way. But this kind of thinking can lead to severe burnout.

If you find yourself saying "yes, but..." to the following questions, you may be caught in "the only one" syndrome:

1. Do you get emotional nourishment from being needed and indispensable?

2. Do you only feel appreciated by the person you help?

3. Is your caregiving responsibility the only role in your life where you feel important?

4. Are you "the only one" because you fear you will be disinherited?

These are just a few of the often unspoken or unconscious traps that can keep a caregiver in an unhealthy over-caring role. If you answered yes to all the questions, consider seeking individual counseling to help develop boundaries and learn how to care for yourself.

To continue caring for someone with a progressive disorder or whose dependence is growing, you will need to acknowledge your feelings honestly. Find a support group with a professional leader. Take classes that expose you to all of the support resources for elders in your community.

If you are unable to find a local support group or professional to talk to, try to find a geriatric care manager who will do a phone consultation.

The following activities may help to prevent "the only one" syndrome:

- Keep a journal with two columns. In one column, write what you have done for your parent. In the other column, write what you have done for yourself—reading a book, eating lunch with a friend, or taking a walk in the park. This will help you compare what you have given and what you have done for self-care. The first step in breaking through resistance is to acknowledge it, then work on finding solutions that give a more balanced approach to life and your caregiving role.

- If Mom or Dad is effusive with their compliments and appreciation, that can hook you into over-caring. If you have a hard time communicating limits, active listening can help. For example, if your older parent says, "You are so wonderful, I don't know what I would do without you," you might respond, "I hear that you appreciate me, Mom." Then add something like "I do the best I can to divide my time between my family, job, self-care, and loving and caring for you." This reminds your parent that you have limits on your time.

- If the caregiving role is the only aspect of your life that makes you feel important or valued, you might need to focus on building other roles and relationships. Your role as caregiver will not go on forever. The best way to help fill the terrible void losing a parent creates is to have other relationships and responsibilities that give your life value and meaning.

- If you find yourself acting as "the only one" because your family member makes threats to disinherit you or write you out of their will, then your caregiving relationship is based more on blackmail than genuine love between a parent and child. If you find yourself in this trap, have a heart-to-heart with yourself and ask, "What will my life be like if I don't receive assets from Mom/Dad's estate?" The reality in many families is that elders live very long lives and need to spend most of their assets on their care. The other reality is if you over-care due to blackmail, you are more likely to suffer from potentially serious health-related issues from stress. In order to continue caring for this type of a parent, you will need to work on limit-setting. (See Chapter Seven: Setting Limits.)

Personal growth often comes at times of high stress, and this might be the time for you to do some self-examination to discover how to enjoy a fuller and more balanced life.

Affirmation:

"I value myself, care for myself,
and find joy in each day."

Part Seven

End-of-Life Decisions and Care

CHAPTER THIRTY-FIVE

Making End-of-Life Decisions

The sad reality is that many families face painful, complicated decisions that affect the length and quality of a parent's life. If the elder's intentions have not been made clear, there can be substantial disagreement among family members about what course to take. Often, everyone involved in decision-making feels overwhelmed and conflicted.

Emotional barriers can prevent opening the end-of-life conversation, but there are tips and tools to ensure your parent's wishes are known and honored.

Every life has a beginning and ending. In our society, work and effort goes into pre-retirement planning, but not into the inevitable decline and death we all face.

As your parent approaches the end of their life, accepting this reality can be hard—no matter if your relationship with them has been troublesome or loving.

The End-of-Life Plan

Without some planning, the end of life can be filled with potholes. But those who have the courage to plan can anticipate or avoid many of them.

Have a healthy conversation and end-of-life planning process by using these simple ideas:

- Understand your parent's wishes. Are these wishes written down, possibly in the form of an advance care directive (ACD) that includes a durable power of attorney for health care decisions (DPOA)? These forms vary from state to state.

- If you have an attorney draw up a customized document, be specific about everything, from treatment options to what type of bedding your parent prefers.

- Unless an attorney customizes the DPOA, it does not usually address preferences for funeral services, burial, or cremation. Five Wishes is a form that does specify these preferences.

- The DPOA names someone ("the agent") to make decisions for your parent. They need to have a conversation—while your parent is still well—about things like tube feedings, hospice, comfort care, etc. Also discuss preferences such as music, sunlight, gardening, pets, or what your parent wants in their environment as they get closer to the end of life.

- The Physician Orders for Life-Sustaining Treatment (POLST) is the form that emergency medical teams follow when determining whether to withhold or accelerate care in a crisis or emergency. These forms can also differ from state to state.

- Many individuals have clear views on the religious rituals they want or don't want. Don't assume because someone is of one faith that they actually want what that faith's tradition might be. Ask: Do you want a funeral mass? Do you want a memorial service? If so, what would you like sung or read at that service? In some religious traditions, it is extremely important to bury the person in a prescribed manner and time frame. Ask those questions and get the directions in writing. Keep this with their legal documents.

- For many people, quality of life matters more than length of life. If you need to make a decision near the end of someone else's life, make that decision based on their values and not your own. If Mom or Dad's quality of life has deteriorated to the point where you feel confident it is not a life they would want to lead, consider hospice or comfort care.

In most states, the forms listed above need to be witnessed but not notarized. A good resource to explore end-of-life care is *Being Mortal,* by Atul Gawande.

The End-of-Life Conversation

Having an end-of-life conversation is never easy, but if you don't know your parent's wishes in advance you will likely be overwhelmed with logistical and emotional dilemmas down the road.

It may help to start the conversation within another conversation. Try something like "We just visited our attorney and he had some great questions for us that I don't know about you." Ask about their wishes, and if they don't have anything in writing, take good notes. Then ask Mom or Dad's permission to give the notes to their attorney so they can be woven into the appropriate documents.

If your parent pushes the conversation away, have a story available that illustrates how life rarely ends suddenly. Try to keep the conversation light, not morbid. Tell them that if and when care is needed, you want to know their wishes, so you don't have to make decisions based on your own likes and dislikes. Ask your parent about preferences that add comfort but differ from individual to individual—such as flannel sheets versus cotton sheets.

If you are still uncomfortable or unable to start this conversation, either have another family member do it, or bring in a professional.

Knowing your parent's wishes and planning accordingly can make their final journey more meaningful, and true to the life they have lived.

Affirmation:

"I have prepared in practical ways for
the end of life and allow the love I feel
today to stay within my heart forever."

CHAPTER THIRTY-SIX

Benefits of Hospice Care

Many families turn to hospice care when the death of a parent is near. Most people who have had an experience with hospice speak highly of their services because it helps elders live alert and pain-free, so they can spend their final days with dignity and quality, surrounded by loved ones.

Though hospice care can occur in an individual home, hospital, nursing home, or private hospice facility, it is a challenging concept for some families. Learn how these services can support your parent and your family—both before and after death—and when to request them.

Most of us have heard of hospice care, but we may not be certain about what it is, who it's for, and when the service should be used. Knowing all of our options for end-of-life care can be empowering and essential to making decisions about the things that are most important to us.

What Is Hospice Care?

Hospice care focuses on people who are in the last stages of a serious illness, usually with an estimated timetable of six months or less to live. If a patient should live longer than an anticipated six months, hospice care does not cease—the supervising physician can initiate a renewal process. This care is not only for diagnoses like cancer or organ failure, but also covers a wide range of ailments like late-stage Alzheimer's disease and dementia.

Hospice is an all-inclusive team approach that includes medical care—medications, equipment, and medical supplies—emotional support, social services, and spiritual resources for those suffering from terminal illness.

During the last stages of an illness, hospice provides pain relief without an intention of curing the illness or prolonging life beyond its natural course. The overall goal is to keep your parent comfortable and improve the quality of their remaining days.

This care is usually provided by loved ones in the comfort of home—your family drives its direction based on Mom or Dad's needs and wishes. A team of nurses, doctors, home care assistants, social workers, clergy, volunteers, and specialists—such as physical, occupational, or speech therapists—gently provides emotional and spiritual support to help everyone in the family prepare for death, and during the grieving process that follows.

When Is It Time for Hospice Care?

Families often wait too long to bring in hospice care because they are hoping for a different outcome. But waiting can cause unnecessary hospitalization, pain, and diminishing quality of life. To secure the highest quality of care for a parent as they approach the end of life, it's important to break through denial and heed the advice of medical professionals.

Selecting a Hospice Provider

Your parent's physician may recommend a hospice program they are familiar with, or you can research the options in your area and make the choice yourself. Be sure to research at least two to three different hospice care providers so you're comfortable with their values and philosophy, as well as their reputation.

Keep in mind that hospice care is often covered by Medicare, Medicaid, or private health insurance.

Affirmation:

"I have confidence that hospice care will be available at the right time."

Glossary

Advance Health Care Directive—an extremely important document to designate an agent to make health care decisions for you when you can't make them. This is not just an end-of-life document but for any health issue that causes you even a short-term disability that impairs your ability to make decisions. It is important to share your values and desires to the person/s you choose to hold this role. Please review the www.PrepareforyourCare.org website for information and a downloadable document you can use, which does not require an attorney to assist you. Every state has somewhat different language that is required for this document, but they all act in the same manner.

Care Manager—not everyone who calls themselves a care manager is truly a professional. This is a term that is not licensed and does not indicate a professional with credentials. Most families want and need a professional geriatric care manager, also called an Aging Life Care Professional˚. This is most often an individual with a master's degree or nursing degree plus at least 5 years' experience with a certification in care management. This individual can be your guide for the entire aging journey or can be used as a consultant to help you make decisions for a specific challenge or to simply age gracefully.

Discharge Manager—a discharge manager is usually a nurse but can be a social worker who works in an acute care hospital to help coordinate your discharge from a hospital. They will arrange for transportation home, home care, and/or medical equipment. Their role ends when you leave the hospital.

Durable Power of Attorney (DPOA)—also called the advanced health care directive or power of attorney for health care. Please see the explanation for advanced health care directive.

Durable Power of Attorney for Finances—a document that must be given to someone you would trust with everything you own. With this power, the person you choose will have access to all property and bank accounts you own that are outside of a trust. They can sell a home, pay your bills, make donations on your behalf. This is a document you do not want to give to someone who is not trustworthy. I would consult legal services or an attorney before giving this power to someone. This document must be notarized. Banks will not automatically accept this document and will most likely send it to their legal departments before acting upon it.

Eldercare Locator—a website that will connect you to a variety of aging services, which are called by different names in different states. They will be able to refer you to local resources that support aging in place, protect seniors, provide legal services and ombudsman, and offer support services for families as well as ideas for social interactions and quality of life. You can access this service by going to www. Eldercare.ACL.gov.

Elder Law Attorney—attorneys that belong to the National Academy of Elder Law Attorneys (NAELA). If you are concerned about qualifying for Medicaid, look for a "Certified Member" of NAELA that specializes in this assistance. Most elder law attorneys are also Estate Planning Attorneys; see www.NAELA.org.

Geriatric Care Manager—also called an Aging Life Care Professional˙ and is a member of the Aging Life Care Association (www.aginglifecare.org). I recommend looking for someone who is an "advanced professional" with at least 5 years of experience. Filter by zip code then level of professional that you require. Aging Life Care Professionals˙ can assist you with most challenges, but some specialize in working with certain diseases or conditions. They can be your long-term resource for you and your aging family member.

Geriatric Pharmacist—a pharmacist that is certified to review medications for efficacy as well as interactions and adverse reactions. The right geriatric pharmacist can be very helpful to families who have family members with more than four prescriptions or those who have had negative responses to medications. Be sure to find a board-certified pharmacist.

Hospital-ready Packet—a packet with the names of medical providers, medications taken, the names of pharmacies used, plus a health history will make any hospitalization much more successful and help the receiving medical team in an emergency room. If you can, prepare a packet with an extra pair of glasses, slippers, and bathrobe. Also remember to bring hearing aids, watch, and/or a cell phone for your family member to stay connected, especially if they restrict visitors for any reason. The packet should also have a copy of the advance health directive and the names and phone numbers of those who will be the advocates.

Living Trust—a legal document drawn up by an attorney. It will hold most of your property and financial accounts and is used to avoid probate taxes and to make your wishes known should you become incapacitated. It also makes it much easier for a chosen trustee to settle the estate of a deceased family member. You should check the document annually to see if you need to make adjustments or changes. The probate codes differ from state to state, so it is best you consult with an estate attorney.

Office on Aging—the Office on Aging is a department in every state that is funded by the federal government and can be called something other than the "Office on Aging" or "Adult & Aging Services." You can find this helpful office at Eldercare.ACL.gov. They most often will refer you to nonprofit providers.

Ombudsman—a service that provides a professional advocate to assist those who live in licensed skilled nursing and/or assisted living facilities. When a service appears to be lacking, abuse is suspected, or families are being unreasonable, the ombudsman can step in to be the advocate for the patient/resident, and find a compromise to ensure the highest quality of life possible. This is funded by the federal government and is available in every state. The Eldercare Locator office will be able to connect you to the ombudsman in your area.

Physician Orders for Life-Sustaining Treatment (POLST)—a document that allows individuals to indicate if they do not want life-sustaining treatment, want just a little, or want everything possible done to keep them alive. It is a document that needs to be signed by the patient or the patient's advocate under an advance health care/power of attorney for health care, and it needs to be signed by the patient's physician. In some states it is called the "Do Not Resuscitate" form.

Power of Attorney for Medical Decisions—see advance health care directive.

Professional Advocate—this term can be many things and needs to be explained and backed up with credentials. Aging Life Care Professionals˚ are such because they have a Standard of Practice, a code of ethics, and high standards for membership. There are other such organizations that also have a history of certification—such as the Case Management Society of America. Elder law attorneys and some mediators consider themselves to be professional advocates. However, some organizations only require a 40-hour class, and not a professional degree—so do your research before hiring someone that calls themselves a professional advocate.

Professional Geriatric Care Manager (PGCM)—these professionals were once a part of the National Association of Professional Geriatric Care Managers and are now members of the Aging Life Care Association. Most members serve all ages, not just geriatric—thus helping individuals with progressive illnesses, those born with lifelong challenges, and the aging population. See a full description under geriatric care manager.

Transitional Care Manager—this can be a professional in a hospital or an insurance system assisting the patient with their transitions from one setting to another. This is for a single event only and not a long-term relationship.

Resources

This is a dynamic list—organizations change over time. So, if you find a dead end in any search, remember to reach out to a geriatric care manager/Aging Life Care Professional® in your family member's location and ask about current local resources—they are being newly created often.

One community might have special programs for seniors that other communities don't offer. That is why it is imperative you connect with someone local when seeking resources.

Navigators

Aging Life Care Professionals® (geriatric care managers—locate professional advocates by your zip code). They can be your eyes and ears and your coach for the entire aging journey. Go to www.aginglifecare.org

Legal

National Academy of Elder Law Attorneys: go to www.Naela.org.

Your community's elder law services (often free or low-cost): go to www.eldercare.acl.gov.

General Information on Illnesses/ Family Caregiving/Community Resources

Family Caregiver Alliance at www.caregiver.org

Alzheimer's Association at www.alz.org

National Institute on Aging at www.nia.nih.gov

Eldercare Locator (locate community resources by zip code) at www.eldercare.acl.gov

Support Groups for Families

Alzheimer's Association (support groups throughout the country) at www.alz.org

Better Health While Aging/Helping Aging Parents at www.betterhealthwhileaging.net

Many churches and senior centers throughout the country have support programs.

Resources and Entitlements

Check for entitlements at www.BenefitsCheckup.org

Medicare at www.Medicare.gov

Social Security at www.SSA.gov

Veterans' benefits at www.va.gov

Moving and Relocation

National Association of Senior Move Managers at www.nasmm.org

Life Care Centers of America for Continuing Care at http://lcca.com

For locating senior housing, use a local Aging Life Care Professional at www.aginglifecare.org, or ask the local Eldercare Locator office for a business in your area. Free placement agencies receive large payments from assisted living. Professionals work just for you and usually charge an hourly fee.

End-of-Life Support

National Hospice & Palliative Care Organization at www.caringinfo.org

Compassion & Choices (planning for care) at www.compassionandchoices.org/end-of-life-planning

Aging with Dignity (planning and end-of-life wishes) at www.fivewishes.org

Prepare for Your Care (creating a health care directive) at
www.prepareforyourcare.org/advance-directive

Scams and Abuse

National Adult Protective Services Association (local APS numbers
you can get from Eldercare Locator) at www.napsa-now.org

National Do Not Call Registry (stop unwanted sales calls) at
www.donotcall.gov

AARP Fraud Watch Network (sign up to receive free alerts) at
www.aarp.org/fraudwatchnetwork

Technology

To research technology from emergency response systems to alert
systems and video calling, go to www.AgeinPlaceTech.com

Enrichment

Villages—Throughout the country we have grassroots senior
villages to keep seniors in their own homes with volunteer support for handyman work, rides, socialization, education, and
peer-to-peer support. To find a low-cost senior village:
https://www.vtvnetwork.org

Hummingbird Project—a therapeutic activity program with trained specialists at

https://hummingbirdproject.net/about-the-hummingbird-project/

Covia—https://covia.org

Well Connected—addresses the issue of loneliness through the mutual support and reciprocal relationships provided by members as well as professionals through online classes

Acknowledgments

I would like to acknowledge and thank the following people for their extraordinary help in bringing this book to life: My husband, Bruce Johnson; my executive assistant at Eldercare Services, Susie Richardson; my business advisor, Ned Rowe; early creation editor, Andrew Schwartz; my daughter, Lauri Taylor, for her business expertise; and all the clients and friends who had been encouraging me to write this book.

About the Author

Linda Fodrini-Johnson became a licensed family therapist and professional certified care manager in 1984, was president of the National Association of Professional Geriatric Care Managers—now called Aging Life Care Association—and founded Eldercare Services, a full-service care agency in the San Francisco Bay Area that provides care management, home care/caregiving services, advocacy, counseling, support groups, and education. She was director of the Dementia Respite Center—one of the first in the San Francisco Bay Area—and pioneered the multi-award-winning Early Stage of Dementia Program.

Her eldercare expertise has been featured in newspapers like the *Contra Costa Times*, *East Bay Business Times*, and *San Francisco Business Times*, as well as national magazines including *Consumer Reports*, *Forbes*, *Kiplinger's*, *USA Today*, and *The Wall Street Journal*. Her book *7 Steps to a Healthy Life for You and Your Aging Parents* is available on Amazon.com.

Linda encourages long-life preparation with quality-of-life as the rudder. To that end, she teaches classes and gives presentations on healthy aging, dementia, family caregiving, as well as end-of-life planning and promotes the value of professional geriatric care management/aging life care experts.